ROLE OF MESENCHYMAL STEM CELLS IN COMMON CLINICAL CONDITIONS

STEM CELLS AND COMMON AILMENTS

MUDASIR BASHIR GUGJOO

Made with ♥ on the Notion Press Platform
www.notionpress.com

Dedicated to all the Scientific personnel

who work day and night

to enlighten us and make our life worth living

....

Contents

Preface

The current monograph is a literature review aimed to keep the readers abreast with the information on advanced therapeutics currently being evaluated for common clinical ailments. The literature in this book aims to detail and/or discuss potential therapeutic applications of the mesenchymal stem cells (MSCs) in common conditions of humans and animals. The clinical conditions chosen are very common, affecting an extensive population in our society. MSCs due to their characteristic properties are considered to provide an all-in-one therapeutic potential and thus, tailor their response as per the clinical ailments. Veterinary sciences make an important component in the development of therapeutics both for humans and animals. Therefore, research in veterinary sciences develops therapeutics for animals and simultaneously provide proof-of therapeutic principle for human medicine. In this edited book, an overview of the diseases is given followed by the limitations of the current therapeutics. The potential role that MSCs can play in control or management of these ailments is discussed vis-a-vis their characteristic properties. The limitations associated with the MSCs are also discussed to make out reasons for their limited success in current scenario. The contents of the chapters however, may not be provide indepth details and information provided may not be that critically analysed.

Acknowledgements

The contents in this compilation is provided by the trainees that underwent SERB sponsored High End Workshop entitled "Mesenchymal Stem Cells in Veterinary Regenerative Medicine". During the training programme, participant were assigned the topics as per their choice and research interest. Considering the trainees as the learners, the monograph may not be expected to provide indepth understanding of the role of MSCs in the conditions enrolled in this monograph. However, their efforts in producing this piece is really appreciable and I am really thankful to all of them. It is pertinent to mention here that the idea for compilation of this monograph has been conceived by the Hon'ble Vice Chancellor of SKUAST-Kashmir, Prof Nazir Ahmad Ganai. The Hon'ble sir has been kind enough to deliberate over the topic and gives his valuable suggestions and idea to draft the hard work of the participants enrolled in the high end workshop. The editor and the authors of the piece are highly thankful to the Hon'ble sir for conceiving this idea. The editor is also really thankful to the SERB-DST, GoI for providing the platform of such a kind. I am also thankful to the colleagues at division of the Veterinary Clinical complex who help me in one way or the other. The special thanks goes to the scientific community that burn their midnight oil to undertake cutting-edge research that makes the contents of the piece.

Words fall short when it comes to the family that stands by you in thick and thin. They are the ones who actually sacrifice when you are dwelled into scientific research. I am really indebted to my parents, better half and children who make my stay comfortable at home and allow me to do something fruitful, like this work, for the society.

Finally, I supplicate to almighty ALLAH (SWT), the ONE (SWT) who listens and responds to supplications, to guide me to the right path, of those on whom YOU (SWT) have bestowed YOUR favors, not of those upon whom YOU (SWT) have incurred YOUR wrath, nor of those who have gone astray, and let not me die except in the state of pure submission to YOU (SWT) alone". Aameen ya rabbal alameen.

Abbreviations

OA: Osteoarthritis; HGF: Hepatocyte growth factor; TGF-β: Transforming growth factor–β; IGF: Insulin-like growth factor; FGF: Fibroblast growth factor; PDGF: Platelet-derived growth factor; MSCs: Mesenchymal stem cells; VEGF: Vascular endothelial growth factor; HO-1: Heme oxygenase; NO: Nitric oxide; IDO: Indoleamine 2,3-dioxygenase; PGE2: Prostaglandin E2; IL: Interleukin; DCs: Dendritic cells; CCL: CC-chemokine ligand; NKs: Natural killer cells; CXCR: C-X-C chemokine receptor type; Nrf2: Nuclear factor erythroid-related factor 2; HIF: Hypoxia-inducible factor; SDF: Stromal cell-derived factor; ANG1: Angiogenesis 1; MCP-1: Monocyte chemotactic protein-1; ROS: Reactive oxygen species; hCAP: Human cathelicidin anti-microbial peptide; MMPs: matrix metalloproteinases; MHC: Major Histocompatibility Complex; EGF: Epidermal growth factor; FGF: Fibroblast growth factors; IGF: Insulin-like growth factors; KGF: Keratinocyte growth factor, NGF: Nerve growth factor, PDGF: Platelet-derived growth factor; TGF: Transforming growth factor; VEGF: Vascular endothelial growth factor, HGF: Hepatocyte growth factor; TNF: Tumor Necrosis Factor; GM-CSF: Granulocyte Monocyte Colony Stimulating Factor; MCP1: Macrophage chemoattractant protein 1; MIP1: Macrophage inflammatory protein 1; MI: Myocardial Infarction; LV: Left ventricle; SDF-1: Stromal derived factor 1; RNA: Ribonucleic acid; miRNAs: mircro RNAs; EF: ejection fraction; FS: fractional shortening; LVESP: LV end systolic pressure; dp/dtmax: Maximal rate of rise of (usually) left ventricular pressure (LVP); LVDd: Left ventricular diameter during diasystole, LVEDV: LV end diasystolic volume; LVEDP: LV end diasystolic pressure; PCO: posterior capsular opacification; EMT: epithelial-mesenchymal transition; LECs: polarized lens epithelial cells; RT-PCR: Real time polymerase chain reaction; ROR1: Receptor tyrosine kinase like orphan receptor 1; SCI: Spinal cord injury; HSP: Heat shock proteins; CD: Cluster of Differentiation; MV: Microvesicles; MDMs: Monocyte-derived macrophages; MARCO: Macrophage receptor with collagenous structure (MARCO); BSCB: Blood-spinal cord barrier; AMR: Antimicrobial resistance; AMP: Antimicrobial peptides; MDR: Multidrug-resistant; XDR: extensively drug-resistant; WHO: World Health Organization; CDC: Centres for Disease Control and Prevention; CRISPR/ Cas: Clustered regularly interspaced short palindromic repeats; LPS: Lipopolysaccharide; MSC-CM:

MSC conditioned medium; OA: Osteoarthritis; NLRP3: NLR family pyrin domain containing 3;TNFR1: Tumor necrosis factor receptor 1; GSDMD: Gasdermin D; PAI-1: Plasminogen activator inhibitor-1; CRP: C-reactive protein; T2DM: Type 2 Diabetes mellitus; ROS: Reactive oxygen species; Mets: Metabolic syndrome; DC: Diabetic cardiomyopathy; DN: Diabetic nephropathy; GVHD: Graft versus host disease; IVDD: intervertebral disc degeneration; DDDs: Degenerative disc diseases; AF: Annulus fibrosis; CEPs: cartilaginous end plates; NP: nucleus pulposus; ISCT: International Society for Cellular Therapy; TRAIL: TNF Related Apoptosis Inducing Ligand; AD: Alzheimer's disease; QoL: quality of life; PRRs: protein recognition receptors); NFTs: neurofibrillary tangles; ESCs: embryonic stem cells; iPSCs: induced pluripotent stem cells; GDNF: Glial cell derived neurotrophic factor; TNT: Tunneling nanotube; MS: Multiple sclerosis

CHAPTER ONE

Mesenchymal Stem Cells for Chronic Wound

Anjum Sabba[1] and **Mudasir B Gugjoo**[2]

[1]*Department of Biochemistry, University of Kashmir, Hazratbal, Srinagar, J&K, India*

[2]*Veterinary Clinical Complex, FVSc & AH, SKUAST-K, Shuhama, J&K, India*

Abstract

Chronic wound is characterized by the delay or failure in healing process to recover the wound to its pre injury state, which sometimes tolls upon the healthcare system as well. Therefore, chronic wound healing becomes a great challenge for clinicians to manage. Researchers are now-a-days exploring cell based therapies for efficient and rapid result oriented approach to combat chronic wound healing problem. Among cell-based therapies, regenerative cell based technique especially mesenchymal stem cells (MSCs) therapy is considered to be more efficient and result oriented. MSCs cannot be utilized as a universal therapy due to some limitations associated with its cellular property. The current chapter details MSCs potential in chronic wound healing.

Key words: Healing Mesenchymal stem cells; Chronic Wound; Scarless healing; Immunomudulation;

Introduction

Wound healing is a complex process which is directed and regulated by signal producing moieties predominantly cytokines and growth factors at the site of injury. The end target of healing is the production of same kind of tissue which has been damaged at the site of injury and which possesses similar characteristics with regard to anatomy and functional integrity. The main process of normal healing is basically an overlapping series of events which has been categorized into three stages (inflammation, proliferation and remodeling). Any alteration or deviation in this process of repair, results in delayed or failed wound healing which otherwise would have been achieved within stipulated time and is technically a chronic wound. Chronic wounds generally lack sufficient skin or granulation tissue bed for closure. Various forms of chronic wounds have been found in animals ranging from epidermal wounds, infected wounds, ulcers to fistula etc (Lux, 2022).

Factors Contributing to the Chronicity of the Wound

Some of the factors which contribute to the chronic wound formation are (Lux, 2022):

- Location (Pressure, trauma and/or lower extremity wounds especially in human and horses)
- High levels of bacterial load
- High levels of inflammatory cytokines
- Excessive reactive oxygen species and proteases in the form of degraded growth factors, matrix metalloproteinases (MMPs), degraded cell surface structures etc
- Aberrant cells/aged cells
- Metabolic diseases
- Medications like immunosuppressant, corticosteroids and anti-inflammatory drugs etc
- Malnutrition

Markers Associated with Chronic Wound

Wound healing studies has been initially reported using animal models. The majority of studies are performed in either rodents, rabbits or pigs. Development of chronic wound differs in humans and animals, although it resembles in them in many ways and thus provide valuable insights across the species in the management of wound healing. Markers associated with chronic wound healing are categorised into three main categories (Gunasekaran et al. 2020; Bodas & Shinde, 2021):

1. **Biochemical markers:** Biochemical markers are chosen from the exudate of chronic wound, which contains a number of inhibitory and activating factors. Increased levels of matrix metalloproteinases (MMP's), proinflammatory cytokines and decreased levels of growth factors are considered potential biochemical markers of chronic wound.

2. **Physiological markers:** Physiological markers of chronic wounds include dermal blood flow via non-invasive laser doppler imaging, wound surface pH, tissue oxygen measurement, wound ultrasonography, transcutaneous oxygen measurement and two biomechanical parameter durometry (for assessment of tissue hardness) and extentsiometry (for assessment of viscoelasticity) respectively.
3. **Tissue markers:** Histological examination has led to number of factors that has been considered as biomarkers like wound infection, dermal collagen, elastin content wound microflora and epithelialization. Micro-array analysis has also been utilised to assess gene activation/ inhibition to predict healing outcomes.

Advanced Therapeutic Approach for Chronic Wound Healing

Traumatic wounds other than chronic ones are generally treated with same basic principles of wound management protocol that will lead to quick healing process. But as far as chronic wound is considered it has a great impact on patient and owner due to long stay in the hospital and prolonged treatment which may sometimes become burden on healthcare system also (Gugjoo et al. 2022; Malhotra et al. 2022). Chronic open wound requires long term treatment because of its delayed primary wound closure and may sometimes tell upon the financial condition of the owner as well. Therefore, chronic wound healing becomes a great challenge for clinicians to manage (Gugjoo, 2022). Presently clinicians are rapidly shifting their wound management protocol from conventional therapies to more advanced cell-based therapies. Among the cell-based therapies, regenerative medicine is currently being regarded as modern and advanced therapy for chronic wound healing as it provides targeted healing in short span of time as compared to conventional therapy and reduces patient morbidity. The main component in regenerative medicine is stem cells especially mesenchymal stem cell (MSC). Mesenchymal stem cells are considered as better therapeutic tool by clinicians because of its ubiquitous nature, multipotency and multi lineage property (Samsonraj et al. 2017; Fabre et al. 2019). The secretome of MSCs play a significant role in suppressing tissue inflammation, immunomodulation, immunogenicity which usually is low (due to lack of MHC class II antigen expression), aiding angiogenesis and assisting in scar-free wound healing (Hu et al. 2018) by exuding cytokines, miRNA, micro vesicles, and exosomes in its immediate microenvironment (da Silva Meirelles et al. 2008; Arevalo-Turrubiarte et al. 2019). Therefore, MSCs have attracted much interest and efforts are being put to harness the capabilities of MSCs for efficient wound healing especially which leads more towards stable pre injury state of the wound (**Fig. 1.1**). Chronic wounds develop due to the combined effect of impaired cellular activity, continuous pro-inflammatory state, growth factor release, deficient matrix synthesis, and reduced neovascularization. Prolonged inflammation, unless not treated well within stipulated time, hampers wound healing under normal circumstances which in long run leads to patient morbidity (Joseph et al. 2021). MSC's being present all over the body can be isolated mostly from bone marrow (BM-MSC), adipose tissues (AD-MSC), periosteum, tendon, muscles etc (Arevalo-Turrubiarte et al. 2019) and from other unconventional sources like amniotic fluid, umbilical cord blood–derived MSCs. In addition to localized function at the site of injury, MSCs bear the ability to home and influence tissue repair at distant locations also. This property of MSCs can be utilised to administer it intravenously or via skeletal muscles especially, in cases presented with condition like myocardial infarction (Mansilla et al. 2005; Lee et al. 2009; Shabbir et al. 2010; Isakson et al. 2015).

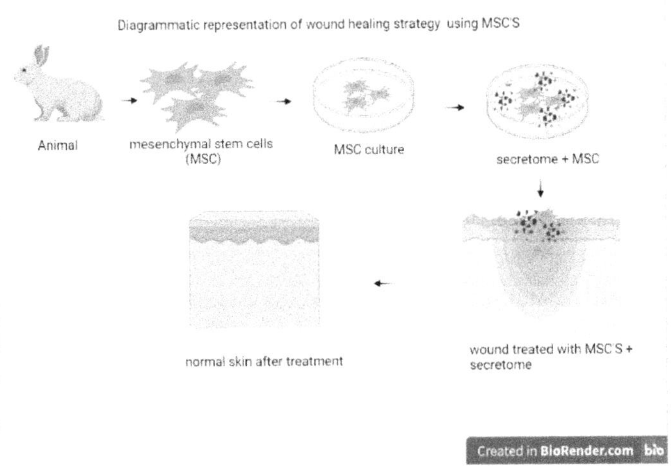

Fig. 1.1: Diagramatic representation of wound healing strategies utilizing mesenchymal stem cells

Secretome Component of MSCs

Secretome component of MSCs plays a crucial role in determining the path taken by the cell and includes the following main factors:

1. **Growth factors:** A number of growth factors like Epidermal growth factor (EGF), Fibroblast growth factors (FGF), Insulin-like growth factors (IGF), Keratinocyte growth factor (KGF), Nerve growth factor (NGF), Platelet-derived growth factor (PDGF), Transforming growth factor (TGF), Vascular endothelial growth factor (VEGF), Hepatocyte growth factor (HGF) and angiopoietin released from MSCs help in proliferation, angiogenesis, re-epithelization, chemotaxis, tissue remodelling, wound closure and inflammation regulation which plays an important role in quick heal response in chronic wounds (Morescalchi et al. 2013).
2. **Cytokines**: cytokines play a vital role in Proliferation, differentiation, chemotaxis, inhibition of scar formation, anti-microbial and anti-inflammatory response. Some of the common cytokines released by MSCs are Interlukin 1 (IL1), Interlukin 6 (IL6), Interlukin 10 (IL10), Interlukin 4 (IL4), Tumor Necrosis Factor (TNF), Gnanulocyte Monocyte Colony Stimulating Factor (GM-CSF), etc (Morescalchi et al. 2013).
3. **Chemokines**: chemokines especially help in migration of macrophages at the site of injury. Besides it also helps in wound closure, re-epithelization etc. it includes Interleukin 8 (IL8), Macrophage chemoattractant protein 1 (MCP1), Macrophage inflammatory protein 1 (MIP1), etc (Tonnesen et al. 2000; Morescalchi et al. 2013).

Furthermore, these MSCs help in the reduction of reduce neutrophil infiltration which in turn decreases neutrophil extracellular trap formation (Sukpat et al. 2020). Keeping in view the multi-tasking property of MSCs it is assumed, that key therapeutic effect of MSCs resides in their paracrine activity on the local environment, thus helping angiogenesis and re-epithelization at the site of chronic wound (Luo et al. 2010; Lee et al. 2012; Schlosser et al. 2012; Fui et al. 2019).

Cell free components of mesenchymal stem cells as considered therapeutic agent. Since the secretome of MSCs includes, micro RNAs, proteasomes, growth factors, cytokines, chemokines, antioxidants, exosomes and micro vesicles etc and play a vital role in healing wounds. The regenerative property of these cells is achieved by either using conditioned media which is the media used for cell growth or extracellular vesicles like exosomes (Fui et al. 2019).

Challenges to Use Mesenchymal Stem Cells as Therapeutic Agent

The use of MSCs as therapeutic agents depends upon different sources from where the MSCs have been derived, different harvesting procedures used which in turn lead to variation in the outcome of cell based therapies. MSCs isolated from different sources cause fluctuations in their differentiation potential, cell passaging number capability and immunomodulatory effect. Therefore, no universal standard protocol for the utilization of MSC based regenerative cell-based therapy has been developed so far (Hass et al. 2011). That is why it becomes a crucial step to select a suitable source for implementation of MSC as a therapeutic agent. Variations in rate of proliferation, differentiation and shot life span of MSCs in *in-vitro* conditions also critically influence MSC-based cell therapies. Besides many secretome products of MSCs have short half-life span which makes the data variable. Few other factors that needs thorough consideration includes batch variation, ideal number and time of MSC implantation, cellular migration and survival time at site of wound, requirement of recurrent implantations, and possibility of controlling and monitoring secretome of MSCs (Fui et al. 2019; Mansoor et al. 2019).

References

1. Arevalo-Turrubiarte M, et al. (2019). Analysis of mesenchymal cells (MSCs) from bone marrow, synovial fluid and mesenteric, neck and tail adipose tissue sources from equines. Stem Cell Res 37: 101442.
2. Bodas K, & Shinde V. (2021). Healing of wounds: a detailed review on models, biomarkers, biochemical and other wound assessment parameters. Inflammation, 9(3).
3. da Silva Meirelles L, et al. (2008). In search of the in vivo identity of mesenchymal stem cells. Stem Cells 26: 2287–99.
4. Fabre H, et al. (2019). Characterization of different sources of human MSCs expanded in serum-free conditions with quantification of chondrogenic induction in 3D. Stem Cells Int Article ID 2186728.
5. Fui LW, et al. (2019). Understanding the multifaceted mechanisms of diabetic wound healing and therapeutic application of stem cells conditioned medium in the healing process. J Tissue Eng Regen Med 13: 2218–33.

6. Gugjoo MB. (2022). Mesenchymal Stem Cells Therapeutic Applications in Integumentary System Disorders. In: Therapeutic Applications of Mesenchymal Stem Cells in Veterinary Medicine. Springer, Singapore.
7. Gugjoo MB, et al. (2022). Cryopreserved Allogeneic Bone marrow Mesenchymal Stem Cells show Better Osteochondral Defect Repair Potential than Adipose Tissue Mesenchymal stem cells. Current Res Transl Med 2022: 103364.
8. Gunasekaran S, et al. (2020). Wound healing potentials of herbal ointment containing Calendula officinalis Linn. On the alteration of immunological markers and biochemical parameters in excision wounded animals. Clin Phytosci 6: 77.
9. Hass R, et al. (2011). Different populations and sources of human mesenchymal stem cells (MSC): a comparison of adult and neonatal tissue-derived MSC. Cell Commun Signal 9: 12.
10. Hu MS, et al. (2018). Mesenchymal stromal cells and cutaneous wound healing: a comprehensive review of the background, role, and therapeutic potential. Stem Cells Int. 2018: 1–13.
11. Isakson M, et al. (2015). Mesenchymal stem cells and cutaneous wound healing: current evidence and future potential. Stem Cells Int 2015: 1–12.
12. Joseph A, et al. (2020). Mesenchymal stem cell-conditioned media: A novel alternative of stem cell therapy for quality wound healing. J Cell Physiol 235: 5555–69
13. Lee RH, et al. (2009). Intravenous hMSCs improve myocardial infarction in mice because cells embolized in lung are activated to secrete the anti-inflammatory protein TSG-6. Cell Stem Cell 5: 54–63.
14. Lee SH, et al. (2012). Paracrine effects of adipose-derived stem cells on keratinocytes and dermal fibroblasts. Ann Dermatol 24: 136.
15. Luo G, et al. (2010). Promotion of cutaneous wound healing by local application of mesenchymal stem cells derived from human umbilical cord blood. Wound Repair Regen 18: 506–13.
16. Lux CN. (2022). Wound healing in animals: a review of physiology and clinical evaluation. Vet Dermatol 33: 91-e27.
17. Malhotra P, et al. (2022). Mesenchymal stem cells are prospective novel off-the-shelf wound management tools. Drug Delivery and Translational Research, 12(1), 79-104.
18. Mansilla E, et al. (2005). Human mesenchymal stem cells are tolerized by mice and improve skin and spinal cord injuries. Transplant Proc 37:

292–4.

19. Mansoor H, et al. (2019). Current trends and future perspective of mesenchymal stem cells and exosomes in corneal diseases. Int J Mol Sci 20: 2853.
20. Morescalchi F, et al. (2013). Proliferative vitreoretinopathy after eye injuries: an overexpression of growth factors and cytokines leading to aretinal keloid. Mediators Inflamm 2013: 1–12.
21. Samsonraj RM, et al. (2017). Concise review: multifaceted characterization of human mesenchymal stem cells for use in regenerative medicine. Stem Cells Transl Med. 6: 2173–85.
22. Schlosser S, et al. (2012). Paracrine effects of mesenchymal stem cells enhance vascular regeneration in ischemic murine skin. Microvasc Res 83: 267–75.
23. Shabbir A, et al. (2010). Activation of host tissue trophic factors through JAK-STAT3 signaling: a mechanism of mesenchymal stem cell-mediated cardiac repair. Am J Physiol Circ Physiol 299: H1428-38.
24. Sukpat S, et al. (2020). Low dose of simvastatin enhanced the therapeutic efficacy of mesenchymal stem cell (MSC) transplantation in skin wound healing in diabetic mice associated with increases in pAkt, SDF-1, and angiogenesistle. bioRxiv 2020.
25. Tonnesen MG, et al. (2000). Angiogenesis in wound healing. J Investig Dermatol Symp Proc 5: 40–6.

CHAPTER TWO

Mesenchymal Stem Cells for Myocardial Infarction

Humaira[1]and **Saba Wani**[2]

[1]Centre of Research for Development (CORD), [2]Department of Biochemistry,

University of Kashmir, Hazratbal, Srinagar, J&K, India

Abstract

Since stem cells especially mesenchymal stem cells have paracrine effects and can modulate the immune system, they represent a viable and cutting-edge therapy approach for heart remodeling. In fact, grafted MSCs have indeed been observed to gather at cardiac damage locales and elicit a variety of impacts, notably Immunomodulation, Angiogenesis, and Myogenesis. The cardiac defensive outcome in ischemic heart disease may be partially explained by the anti-inflammation function of MSC implantation. With their potential to differentiate in multiple directions, minimal immunogenicity, and great portability, marrow stromal cells make excellent seed cells for the therapy of cardiac ailments.

Key words: Mesenchymal stem cells; Myocardial infarction; Regeneration; Remodelling

Introduction

Cardiovascular disease poses a serious health risk to humans on a global scale considering its importance for normal body functioning. In current history, Myocardial Infarction (MI), which continues to be a significant contributor to death, has become a major global public health concern. Cardiomyocytes and other heart cell types unquestionably die at the beginning of MI due to a lack of blood and oxygen. The proportion of surviving cardiocytes decreases after coronary thrombosis or other heart conditions. The capability of the myocardium to contract after a MI decreases due to the development of fibrous scar tissue and cardiac hypertrophy. A recurrence of heart failure as an additional danger to one's life may ultimately occur from the reduction in cardiac function. Despite coronary stents, thrombolysis, and coronary artery bypass grafting having all been utilized to cure MI in clinical settings, nothing of these treatments can undo the damage to the infarcted myocardial nor significantly enhance heart function. Therefore, current line of investigation has focused on discovering a way to enhance heart function by rejuvenation of injured and dysfunctional myocardium. In recent times, researchers have focused heavily on using stem cells to mend injured myocardium and regain heart output. Currently, myocardial ischemia is treated with medicines, procedures, and coronary artery bypass grafting, however, these techniques cannot repair tissue that has been destroyed by MI. The local drop-in cardiocyte numbers in the infarcted area brought on by redox imbalance in the inflammatory milieu, tissue fibrosis, scar tissue generation, and cardiac remodeling are the primary causes of the enhanced incidence of cardiovascular insufficiency and fatality after MI. As a result, scientists have started looking for a fresh approach to treating heart problems following MI. With the help of cardiac stem cells, induced pluripotent stem cells, cardiovascular progenitor cells, peripheral blood stem cells, stromal cells, as well as other stem cell types, stem cell therapy is currently a cutting-edge therapeutic approach that can aid in microvasculature restoration and endorse myocardial compensatory frameworks. Among these stem cell types, mesenchymal stem cells (MSCs), a subset of multipotent germ cells can be primarily extracted from myeloid tissue. Due to their capacity for several directions of differentiation and their low immunogenicity, they have indeed been extensively utilized in cell transplantation therapy throughout the last few decades. A significant origin of stem and progenitor cells is the myeloid tissue. MSCs, also known as medicinal signaling cells, have the capacity to replicate widely, differentiate along a variety of pathways, and give rise to muscle, brain, liver, cartilage, bone, fat, and vessels *in vitro* or *in vivo*, aiding in tissue repair.

Role of stem cells in Myocardial Infarction

Due to their characteristic properties Anti-inflammation, Anti-apoptosis, Immunomodulation, Pro-angiogenesis, and revival, MSCs have received a lot of interest. MSCs offer a seemingly secure and effective way to treat MI. Earlier, primary mechanism for MSC-mediated cardiac treatment was their differentiation to functional cells, including endothelial cells (Gupta et al. 2021). However, mounting research suggest that instead differentiation, MSCs carry out repair functions via alternate mechanisms. This includes the paracrine production of growth hormones and inflammation-regulatory proteins (**Fig. 2.1**) (Li et al. 2009; Sid-Otmane et al. 2020). The use of MSCs as a novel therapeutic archetype to cure myocardial infarction is widely evaluated. Empirical investigations have shown that methods focussing on leukocyte activation/adhesion, macrophage polarisation, or T-cell stimulation are effective in reducing ischemia damage, which has generated a lot of interest in MSC-based MI therapy (Gugjoo, 2022). Recent research has shown that administering a secretome derived from MSCs is a successful method for controlling inflammation in MI. The ability to distribute cytokines, immunomodulatory substances, growth regulators, or ncRNA to target cells is essential for MSCs secretome based positive impacts. Along with the capability for instant accessibility and long-term maintenance, it won't also cause allogeneic immunological reactions and inflammation. Consequently, MSCs secretome will be a fascinating focus that merits additional research in upcoming experiments and clinical trials.

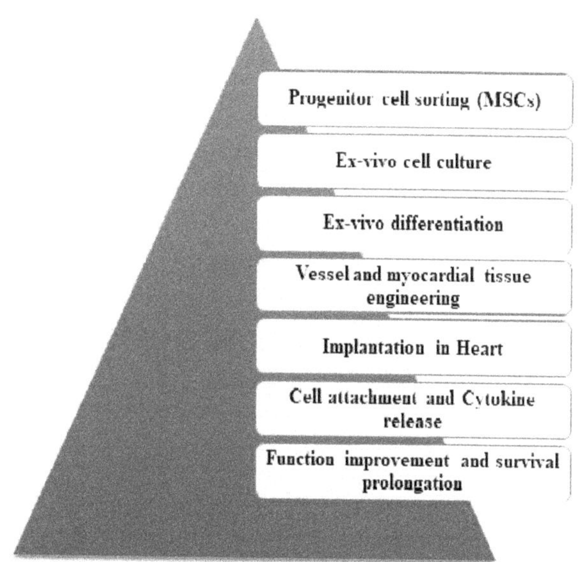

Fig. 2.1: Flowchart of MSCs therapy in Myocardial Infarction

Effects of MSCs on Immune Regulation and Inflammation

Due to minimal transcription of Fas ligand and MHC class I molecules and no transcription of MHC class II molecules, MSCs have the characteristics of minimal immunogenicity and antigen-presenting capacity (Tse et al. 2003). This allows MSCs to decrease T-cell multiplication, leading to immunological exclusion or immune endurance. The paracrine suppression of active inflammatory chemicals and the control of immune cells are the two key components of MSCs immunomodulatory strategy. It is discovered that replacement with MSCs meaningfully upgrade the purpose of the myocardium in a mouse model by significantly lowering the levels of TNF-, IL-1, and IL-6 as well as Cardiocyte mortality (Guo et al. 2007).

Anti-fibrotic effects of MSCs

Numerous cardiocytes perish following MI and are replenished by phagocytes tending to fibrous tissue. Heart disease, a leading cause of cardiovascular mortality, is brought on by left ventricle (LV) remodeling and arrhythmia. By controlling matrix metalloproteinases (MMPs) and inhibitors of matrix metalloproteinases, stromal cells can prevent the stimulation of phagocytes, control of fibrous connective tissue, and other intercellular matrices, hence minimizing LV reshaping and enhancing heart rhythm after myocardial infarction. It has been shown that human hepatocyte growth factor, an eminent anti-fibrosis factor, significantly contributes to the anti-fibrosis activity of MSCs *in-vitro* (Li et al., 2015).

Angiogenesis and the function of BM-MSCs

The formation of large arteries and capillaries is referred to as angiogenesis, a crucial phase in the therapy of MI. When MSCs are implanted into the adjacent infarcted area, they produce an abundance of differentiation factors, including VEGF and SDF-1, which can command angiogenesis and block signaling lanes to encourage the evolution of vasoganglion. miRNAs are involved in the control of vascular compartment distinction, escalation, exodus, and supplementary biochemical characteristics, according to an expanding body of research. Some miRNAs, including miR-126, miR-132, and others, have the capacity to encourage angiogenesis. In a rat model, overexpressed miR-126 controlled the AKT/ ERK signaling pathway to promote angiogenesis all around the infarcted zone (Kim et al., 2012). Another study showed that MSCs given intravenously could engraft in the ischemic myocardium and this could lead to myogenesis and angiogenesis as the embedded MSCs developed into cardiomyocytes and vascular endothelial cells. They also showed that following a severe myocardial infarction in rats, MSC transplantation reduced the extent of the infarct and enhanced heart health (Noritoshi et al., 2004). The therapeutic perspective of transplanting MSCs in myocardial infarction was the subject of another investigation. The primary conclusion of their study is as follows:

(1) In non-infarcted areas, MSC implantation modulated TNF-α, IL-1β, and IL-6 gene expression and protein synthesis.

(2) When MSCs were transplanted, type I and type III collagen accumulation was prevented, matrix metalloproteinase-1 (MMP-1) and tissue inhibitor of matrix metalloproteinase-1 (TIMP-1) production was decreased in non-infarcted areas, and left ventricular performance was enhanced.

(3) After myocardial infarction, myocardial remodeling was prevented post MSCs transplantation. It reduced LV cavitary dilation and transmural infarct flattening.

(4) Improved cardiac activity following MSCs transplantation in the form of increase in EF, FS, LVESP, and dp/dtmax and decreases in LVDd, LVEDV, and LVEDP (Jun et al. 2007).

Following a 2-week MI, the paracrine function of engrafted MSC revealed that:

1) Cardiovascular performance (EF, LVESP, LVEDP, and dp/dtmax) was augmented by MSC implantation.

2) Even just a small number of transplanted cells actively contributed to myocardial discrepancy and angiogenesis, although the capillary density amplified dramatically.

3) Around the site of MSC implantation, VEGF and bFGF mRNA expression and protein synthesis were boosted by MSCs (Zicheng et al. 2009).

Conclusion

Heart failure following Myocardial Infarction (MI) has not been entirely reversed by current medical therapies. Novel treatment approaches are indeed urgently needed for practical application. MSC-based inflammatory control therapy has been shown to be a potential treatment for MI in both experimental and clinical investigations. After an acute MI, MSCs implantation abridged the infarct size and enhanced heart activity by promoting angiogenesis and myogenesis. MSCs implantation may therefore provide a novel therapeutic approach for the management of MI. Although BM-MSCs therapy has been tried, the best dosage and method of administration of BM-MSCs for the cure of MI should be evaluated. The brief cardioprotective impacts of MSC implantation are at least partially explained by the paracrine function. The major limitation with MSCs therapy is their potential to develop foci of arrhythmia.

References

1. Guo J, et al. (2007). Anti-inflammation role for mesenchymal stem cells transplantation in myocardial infarction. Inflammation 30(3–4): 97–104.
2. Gupta S, et al. (2021). Mesenchymal stem cells for cardiac regeneration: from differentiation to cell delivery. Stem Cell Rev Rep 17: 1666–94.
3. Jun G, et al. (2007). Anti-Inflammation Role for Mesenchymal Stem Cells Transplantation in Myocardial Infarction. Inflammation. 30: 3Y4.
4. Gugjoo MB. (2022). Mesenchymal Stem Cells Therapeutic Applications in Cardiovascular Disorders. In: Therapeutic Applications of Mesenchymal Stem Cells in Veterinary Medicine. Springer Nature, pp. 213-245.
5. Kim HW, et al. (2012). Concomitant activation of miR-107/ PDCD10 and hypoxamir-210/Casp8ap2 and their role in cytoprotection during ischemic preconditioning of stem cells. Antioxid Redox Signal 17(8): 1053–65.
6. Li X, et al. (2015). Direct intercellular communications dominate the interaction between adipose-derived MSCs and myofibroblasts against cardiac fibrosis. Protein Cell 6(10): 735–45.
7. Li Z, et al. (2009). Paracrine role for mesenchymal stem cells in acute myocardial infarction. Biol Pharm Bull 32: 1343–6.
8. Noritoshi N, et al. (2004). Intravenous administration of mesenchymal stem cells improves cardiac function in rats with acute myocardial infarction through angiogenesis and myogenesis.Physiol Heart Circ Physiol 287: H2670–H2676.
9. Sid-Otmane C, et al. (2020). Mesenchymal stem cell mediates cardiac repair through autocrine, paracrine, and endocrine axes. J Transl Med 18: 336.
10. Tse WT, et al. (2003). Suppression of allogeneic T-cell proliferation by human marrow stromal cells: implications in transplantation. Transplant 75(3): 301–7.
11. Zicheng L, et al.(2009).Paracrine Role for Mesenchymal Stem Cells in Acute Myocardial Infarction. Biol. Pharm. Bull32(8): 1343—1346.

CHAPTER THREE

Mesenchymal Stem Cells for Cataract

Chaithra S N[1], **Aakanksha**[a]and **Mudasir B Gugjoo**[2]
[1]*Veterinary Surgery, ICAR-IVRI, Izatnagar, Bareilly, UP, India &*
[2]*Veterinary Clinical Complex, FVSc & AH, SKUAST-K, Srinagar, J&K, India*

Abstract

Cataract, the opacification of ocular lens, is the leading cause of blindness worldwide. Although cataract surgery restores vision initially, a common postoperative complication is posterior capsular opacification (PCO). In stem cells therapy for cataract the damaged lens is removed but the outer lens surface which is the lens capsule is left intact and the epithelial stem cells are implanted within the lens capsule to help in repair mechanism. It is hypothesized that the lens capsule could act as a natural scaffold and human Wharton's Jelly mesenchymal stem cells could be used to restore the lens structure in the empty capsule.

Key words: Cataract; Lens capsule; Mesenchymal stem cells; Opacification

Introduction

Cataract, the opacification of ocular lens, is the leading cause of blindness worldwide (Foster et al., 2005). Cataract affects the clear ocular vision and is responsible for 51% of the world's blindness cases affecting 20 million of human population (http://www.who.int/blindness/causes/priority/en/index1.html). It has multiple etiology such as ageing, traumatic ocular injuries, inflammatory or metabolic diseases like diabetes, use of steroid medications. The common pathway involves the breakdown of the lens protein and fibres. These broken proteins and fibers clump together resulting in the cloudiness of the eye. It blocks the light passage and prevents the formation of a sharp image on the retina. There is compelling evidence implicating epithelial-mesenchymal transition (EMT) in the pathogenesis of anterior subcapsular cataract (ASC) and posterior capsular opacification(PCO). During EMT, polarized lens epithelial cells (LECs) relinquish their cobblestone morphology and transdifferentiate into spindle-shaped myofibroblastic cells that elongate and migrate across the lens capsule (**Fig. 3.1**) (de Longh et al., 2005). The clinical signs of blurred vision, difficult night vision, light sensitivity, halos around light, double vision are associated with cataract.

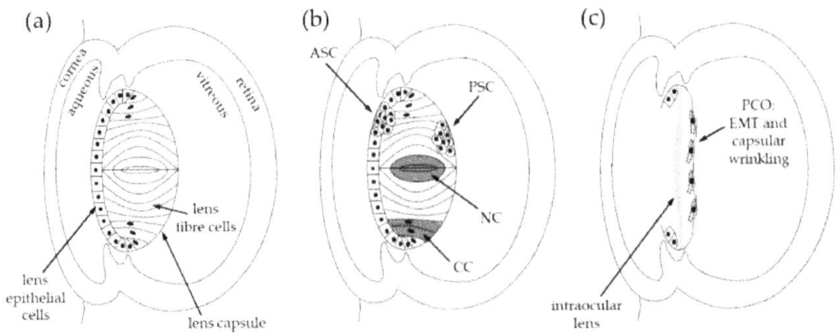

Fig. 3.1: Diagram of lens and cataract types: a) Location of lens and lens epithelial cells (LECs) and lens fibre cells within the eye. Black dots indicate nuclei within the epithelial cells and differentiating fibre cells; b) Location of different types of cataract within the lens, including anterior subcapsular cataract (ASC), posterior subcapsular cataract (PSC), cortical cataract and nuclear cataract (NC); c) Location of posterior capsule opacification PCO) in the lens capsular bag after cataract surgery. Lens epithelial cells undergo epithelial-mesenchymal transition (EMT) and cause capsular wrinkling (Recycled from Dewi and O'Connor, 2019 (CC BY Licence).

The effective surgical procedure involves removal of natural lens and replacement by an artificial lens (Snellingen et al., 2002). Although cataract surgery restores vision initially, a common postoperative complication is PCO that may occur due to the growth and proliferation of remainder epithelial cells thereby interfering with light transmission (O'Connor and Mcavoy, 2007; Maleki et al., 2010). Advances in surgical techniques and intraocular lens design have reduced the prevalence of PCO, yet it remains a significant and uneradicated problem (Awasti et al., 2009). Currently Nd:YAG laser capsulotomy is the only effective treatments for PCO. However, it carries vision-related surgical complications and place major personal and financial burden on the aging population (Awasti et al., 2009). Hence, there is interest in the development of non-invasive pharmacologic alternatives to maintain lens transparency.

The lens capsule is the outer limit which shapes the lens and protects it from bacterial or viral infection by isolating the lens from other ocular tissues (Cotlier et al., 1968; Karkinen et al., 1975; Beyer et al.,1984). The molecular adult lens capsules are composed of networks of laminin, type-4 collagen, entactin/nidogen, several heparin sulphate proteoglycans including perlecan and collagen-13, and possibly collagen-15 and agrin (Ylikärppä et al., 2003). Hence lens capsules can act as a natural scaffold for tissue engineering (Gwon, 2007).

Mesenchymal stem cell therapy in cataract

Cells and tissue based therapeutic procedures are new strategies for this purpose. Therapy with stem cells having a potential to differentiate into the lens fiber cells is a new candidate for the treatment of cataract. Most focused cells for therapeutic concern are pluripotent stem cells and their derivatives. In stem cells therapy for cataract the damaged lens is removed but the outer lens surface which is the lens capsule is left intact and the epithelial stem cells line along the capsule to help in repair mechanism. Contrary to the replacement of damaged lens with an artificial alternative, a natural lens is regrown in stem cells therapy thus, leading to a better vision. Only lower vertebrates have the ability to spontaneously regenerate the ocular lens (Tsonis and DelRio Tsonis, 2004; Barbosa-Sabanero et al., 2012). There are less complications associated with stem cells based cataract management in contrast to the conventional procedures (Gugjoo, 2022) (**Fig. 3.2**). Evans and Fleiszig (2013) reports full lens regeneration in cataract patients' upto a follow up period of 8 months post stem cell therapy.

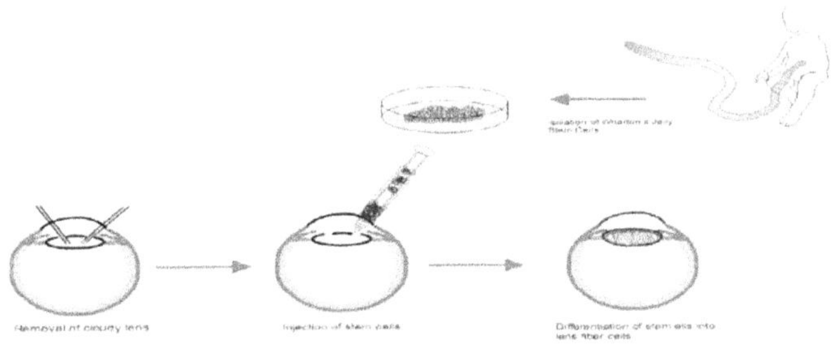

Fig. 3.2: Transplantation of mesenchymal stem cells post cataract surgery(*Recycled from Maleki, 2015 (CC BY Licence)*

Role of Lens Epithelial Cells (LECs) in lens regeneration

At the equator of the mature lens, LECs start to differentiate and cover the anterior surface of the lens, forming translucent, three-dimensional convex lens fibres. One of the most important tasks of LECs is sustained self-renewal and protective capabilities against external harm and oxidative damage (Beebe et al., 2010). Lenticular bodies expressed mature lens-fibre-specific genes encoding for αA-, β-, and γ-crystallins. α and βγ crystallines, as demonstrated by immunostaining and western blot analysis. The hallmarks of lens fibre distinction are crystalline proteins (Maleki et al., 2010; Khatami et al., 2014). Expression of α-A and α-B crystalline leads to the differentiation of human and murine Wharton's jelly stem cells (WJ-MSCs) into lens fibre cells. The expression of the αB-, βB1- and βB3 crystalline genes was confirmed RT-PCR while cell elongation and alignment with neighbouring cells upon electron microscopy (Maleki, 2015).

Lens preservation and lens regeneration

Age-related cataract is still a primary cause of reduced vision and blindness globally, despite the widespread availability of extremely effective surgical therapy (Pascolini & Mariotti, 2012; Wei et al. 2022). Searches for non-surgical ways to postpone, prevent, or reverse cataract formation have been spurred by the continuous ageing of people around the world and the increase in age-related cataract that would inevitably ensue (Taylor, 2000; Toh et al., 2007; Rao et al., 2011; Moreau and King, 2012b).

The receptor tyrosine kinase like orphan receptor 1 (ROR1-LEC)/micro-lens system shares the most functional lens characteristics with primary human lenses, particularly the capacity to focus light. As a result, the emphasis is placed on how the ROR1-LEC/micro-lens combination might be used to study cataract formation. ROR1-expressing LECs were treated to a medication (Vx-770) thought to cause non-congenital cataract in young cystic fibrosis patients in order to see if they might be used to study cataract formation under *in vitro* (Dryden et al., 2016; McColley, 2016). Surprisingly, high Vx-770 concentrations caused micro-lenses to lose their capacity to transmit and focus light (Murphy et al., 2018). These results imply that ROR1-expressing LECs and microlenses generated from human PS cells could help identify the particular, starting cataract molecular pathways resulting from various cataract risk factors. The ability to precisely modify the environment in which human lens cells and microlenses derived from stem cells are cultured—for instance, by varying the oxygen concentration (hypoxia, normoxia, hyperoxia), nutrients, drugs, etc. offers a new opportunity to define how specific factors act alone or in combination to cause cataract initiation and progression. MSCs utilization per se has not been made in large animals in cataract and as such should be taken to understand their role. MSCs clinical applicability, however, has been hampered by a number of issues, including tumorigenicity and immunological rejection. Utilizing endogenous stem/progenitor cells directly for repair and regeneration is an appealing approach.

Conclusion

The lens capsule can serve as the natural framework that creates the lens structure because it is made up of laminin, type IV collagen, entactin/nidogen, perlecan, collagen XVIII, and probably collagen XV and agrin. When placed within an empty capsule, the hWJSCs have the ability to differentiate into lens fibre cells and then rebuild the lens structure. Additionally, human PS-cell-derived lens cells and microlenses, which have a number of morphological, molecular, and functional characteristics with primary human lenses, can serve as a significant source of functional human lens tissue. The current research may contain some predictions about how to cure cataracts, but it should still be tested in clinical studies for safety and efficacy before being adopted as a novel approach for the condition.

References

1. Awasthi N, et al. (2009). Posterior capsular opacification: a problem reduced but not yet eradicated. Arch Ophthalmol 127:555–562.
2. Barbosa-Sabanero K, et al. (2012). Lens and retina regeneration: new perspectives from model organisms. Biochem J 447: 321–334.
3. Beebe DC, et al. (2010). Oxidative damage and the prevention of age-related cataracts. Ophthalmic Res 44: 155–165.
4. Beyer T, et al. (1984). Protective barrier effect of the posterior lens capsule in exogenous bacterial endophthalmitis--an experimental primate study. Invest Ophthalmol Vis Sci 25: 108–12.
5. Cotlier E, et al. (1968). Pathogenic effects of rubella virus on embryos and newborn rats. Nature6: 38–40.
6. de Iongh RU, et al. (2005). Transforming growth factor-beta-induced epithelial-mesenchymal transition in the lens: a model for cataract formation. Cells Tissues Organs 179: 43–55.
7. Dewi CU, & O'Connor MD. (2019). Use of Human Pluripotent Stem Cells to Define Initiating Molecular Mechanisms of Cataract for Anti-Cataract Drug Discovery. *Cells8:* 1269.
8. Dryden C, et al. (2016). The impact of 12 months treatment with ivacaftor on Scottish paediatric patients with cystic fibrosis with the G551D mutation: A review. Arch. Dis. Child 103: 68.
9. Evans DJ, & Fleiszig SM. (2013). Microbial keratitis: could contact lens material affect disease pathogenesis? Eye Contact Lens 39(1): 73.
10. Gugjoo MB. (2022). Mesenchymal Stem Cells Therapeutic Applications in Eye and Adnexa Ailments. In: Therapeutic Applications of Mesenchymal Stem Cells in Veterinary Medicine. Springer Nature. pp. 391-408.
11. Gwon AE. (2007). Controlled ocular lens regeneration. *Google Patents.*
12. http://www.who.int/blindness/causes/priority/en/index1.html.
13. Karkinen-Jääskeläinen M, et al. (1975). Rubella cataract in vitro: Sensitive period of the developing human lens. J Exp Med 141: 1238–48.
14. Khatami S, et al. (2014). Stem Cell Isolation from Human Wharton's Jelly: A Study of Their Differentiation Ability into Lens Fiber Cells. Cell Journal (Yakhteh) 15: 364–71.
15. Maleki M, et al. (2010). Induction of Alpha-crystallins expression in umbilical cord mesenchymal stem cell. IJOR22: 67–71.
16. Maleki M. (2015). Stem cell therapy of cataract. Bioimpacts 5(4): 165-7.
17. McColley S.A. (2016). A safety evaluation of ivacaftor for the treatment of cystic fibrosis. Expert Opin Drug Saf 15: 709–715.

18. Moreau KL, & King JA. (2012). Protein misfolding and aggregation in cataract disease and prospects for prevention. Trends Mol Med 18(5): 273-282.
19. Murphy P, et al. (2018). Light-focusing human micro-lenses generated from pluripotent stem cells model lens development and drug-induced cataract in vitro. Dev 145: dev155838.
20. O'Connor MD, & Mcavoy JW. (2007). In vitro generation of functional lens-like structures with relevance to age-related nuclear cataract. Invest Ophthalmol Vis Sci48: 1245–52.
21. Pascolini D, & Mariotti SP. (2012). Global estimates of visual impairment: 2010. Br J Ophthalmol 96(5): 614-618.
22. Rao GN, et al. (2011). The global burden of cataract. Current Opinion Ophthalmol 22(1): 4-9.
23. Snellingen T, et al. (2002). Surgical interventions for age-related cataract. Cochrane Database of Systematic Reviews, CD00132.
24. Taylor HR. (2000). Cataract: how much surgery do we have to do?. Br J Ophthalmol 84(1): 1-2.
25. Toh TY, et al. (2007). Medical treatment of cataract. Clin Exp Ophthalmol 35(7): 664-671.
26. Tsonis PA, & Del Rio-Tsonis K. (2004). Lens and retina regeneration: transdifferentiation, stem cells and clinical applications. Exp Eye Res 78: 161–172.
27. Wei Z, et al. (2022). Aged Lens Epithelial Cells Suppress Proliferation and Epithelial-Mesenchymal Transition-Relevance for Posterior Capsule Opacification. Cells. 2022: 11(13)
28. Ylikärppä R, et al. (2003). Double knockout mice reveal a lack of major functional compensation between collagens XV and XVIII. Matrix Biol22: 443–8.

CHAPTER FOUR

Mesenchymal Stem Cells for Spinal Cord Injury

Anmol Dhiman and **Jitender Kumar**

Division of Medicine, ICAR-IVRI-Izatnagar, Bareilly, UP, India

Abstract

Spinal cord injury (SCI) is a devastating medical condition with intense socioeconomic impacts. Although there are ongoing researches but current treatment plans are less to restore functionality of injured spinal cord. Many studies suggest that mesenchymal stem cell-derived exosomes (MSC-exosomes) are new treatment for SCI patients. MSCs are self-renewing multipotent stem cells with multi-directional differentiation and can secrete large number of exosomes. These MSC-exosomes play a crucial role in repairing injured spinal cord by enhancing angiogenesis and axonal growth, encourage inflammation and the immune response, inhibiting apoptosis, and keep the integrity of the blood-spinal cord barrier.

Key words: Spinal cord injury; Repair; Mesenchymal stem cells; MARCO antagonist

Introduction

Spinal cord injury (SCI) leads to serious motor and sensory disarrangement of the limbs below the injured segment. Currently, there is no effective treatment procedure, the prevention, treatment and rehabilitation of animals with SCI has become serious problem to be solved. According to definition of the International Spinal Cord Society, SCI is divided into traumatic spinal cord injury and non-traumatic spinal cord injury. Current treatments for SCI include corticosteroids, surgical decompression, hemodynamic therapy and invasive spinal cord pressure monitoring. Although, these methods listed do not fully restore the function of the injured spinal cord, and it is crucial to discover a new treatment plan for treating SCI (Liu and Ma et al., 2021). MSCs offer a hope due to their characteristic properties including anti-inflammatory actions, immunomodulation, differentiation and ability to recruit local prohealing cells. These cells usually operate through their secretome that harbours prohealing proteins, genetic materials and mitochondria (Liu and Ma et al., 2021). There are numerous sources from which MSCs can be harvested, although the properties of the cells may vary depending upon the donor species, tissue and physiology state of the donor.

Mesenchymal stem cell therapy for spinal cord injury

MSCs transplantation is seen to improve symptoms in the SCI models (Gugjoo et al. 2020). There is repairmen reported in both acute and chronic compression models of SCI. However, complete regeneration and recovery remains a big challenge. Compressive SCI models report improvement in behavioural scores and nerve conduction velocity that too as early as 2 weeks post cell transplantation (Gugjoo, 2022). Add-on MSCs transfected with haemoxygenase-1 (HO-1) (Kim et al. 2022) and BDNF (Lee et al. 2016) also potentiate MSCs repair potential in animal models. However, there are lot challenges for MSCs to e utilized as standard therapeutics in SCI.

Bone marrow mesenchymal stem cells (BM-MSCs) derived exosome-induced Macrophages promote the functional healing post SCI (Li and Qin et al., 2021). BM-MSCs cell sheets are able to enhance the functional recovery and alleviate neurogenic pain more effectively than intramedullary injections (Yamazaki and Kawabori et al., 2021). Monocyte-derived macrophages (MDMs) infiltrating into the injured site could efficiently phagocytise myelin debris and process phagocytic material that process however, remains compromised after SCI. The injection of BM-MSCs-exosomes as an option for SCI treatment could protect the macrophage normal functioning by enhancing the phagocytic ability of myelin debries. This has been confirmed by inhibition of macrophage receptor with collagenous structure (MARCO) with PolyG. Such an inhibition weakens the effect of BM-MSCs-exosomes on the phagocytic ability of the macrophages, resulting in compromised myelin clearance at the site of injury and enhanced tissue damage and impairment of the functional healing capacity. Macrophage treatment with BM-MSCs-exos enhances the ability of macrophages to phagocytose myelin debris *in vitro* and make a regenerative microenvironment for axon regrowth (Sheng and Zhao et al., 2021).

One of the studies reveal that combined therapy with transcranial magnetic stimulation and BM-MSCs transplantation or Raf inhibition in spinal cord injury of rat enhances locomotor functional recovery. Moreover, monotherapy leads to suppression of the neuronal apoptosis and promotes axonal regeneration, over and above diminishing astroglial activation in SCI model of rats. Combination therapy leads to decrease in SCI-induced spinal cord lesions and neuronal apoptosis. Therefore, it shows that comparison of monotherapy with combination therapy exhibit an improved curative effect on SCI by further suppressing Raf/MEK/ERK signaling (Feng and Wang et al., 2021). BM-MSCs-derived extracellular vesicles may deliver microRNA-23b to decrease the spinal cord injury by targeting toll-like receptor TLR4 and inhibiting NF-κB pathway activation (Nie H and Jiang Z, 2021). UC-MSCs increase repair of the injured spinal cord tissue and also have an analgesic response by decreasing the secretion of inflammatory factors like IL-6 and TNF-α and upregulating the expression of GD (Wu et al., 2020). In rats (Exo-miR-494) have ability of inhibiting the inflammatory response and neuronal apoptosis in the injured area, over and above upregulating different anti-inflammatory factors and miR-494 to protect neurons. Moreover, it enhances the regeneration of the neurofilament and improve the recovery of behaviour (Huang and Lin et al., 2021).

Conclusion

MSCs are self-renewing multipotent stem cells with multi-directional differentiation and can secrete extracellular vesicles (exosomes) and growth factors. These MSC-derived exosomes play a crucial role in repairing injured spinal cord by enhancing angiogenesis and axonal growth, encourage inflammation and the immune response, inhibiting apoptosis, and keep the integrity of the blood-spinal cord barrier. However, further clinical trials are required to establish their efficacy in clinical cases.

References

1. Feng S, et al. (2021). Effects of combination treatment with transcranial magnetic stimulation and bone marrow mesenchymal stem cell transplantation or Raf inhibition on spinal cord injury in rats. Mol Med Rep 23(4): 294.
2. Gugjoo MB. (2022). Mesenchymal stem cells therapeutic applications in central nervous system disorders. In: Therapeutic applications of mesenchymal stem cells in veterinary medicine. Springer Nature. Pp. 163-212.

3. Gugjoo MB, et al. (2020). Dog Mesenchymal Stem Cell Basic Research and Potential Applications. In: Mesenchymal Stem Cell in Veterinary Sciences. Springer Nature. pp. 213-282.
4. Huang W, et al. (2021). Rat Bone Mesenchymal Stem Cell-Derived Exosomes Loaded with miR-494 Promoting Neurofilament Regeneration and Behavioral Function Recovery after Spinal Cord Injury. Oxid Med Cell Longev 2021:1634917.
5. KimWK, et al. (2022). Heat-Shock Proteins Can Potentiate the Therapeutic Ability of Cryopreserved Mesenchymal Stem Cells for the Treatment of Acute Spinal Cord Injury in Dogs. Stem Cell Rev Rep 18(4):1461-1477.
6. Li C, et al. (2021). Bone Marrow Mesenchymal Stem Cell-Derived Exosome-Educated Macrophages Promote Functional Healing After Spinal Cord Injury. Front Cell Neurosci 15: 725573.
7. Liu WZ, et al. (2021). Mesenchymal stem cell-derived exosomes: therapeutic opportunities and challenges for spinal cord injury. Stem Cell Res Ther 2021 12(1): 102.
8. Liu WZ, et al. (2021). Mesenchymal stem cell-derived exosomes: therapeutic opportunities and challenges for spinal cord injury. Stem Cell Res Ther 12(1): 102.
9. Nie H, & Jiang Z. (2021). Bone mesenchymal stem cell-derived extracellular vesicles deliver microRNA-23b to alleviate spinal cord injury by targeting toll-like receptor TLR4 and inhibiting NF-κB pathway activation. Bioengineered 12(1): 8157-8172.
10. Sheng X, et al. (2021). Bone Marrow Mesenchymal Stem Cell-Derived Exosomes Accelerate Functional Recovery After Spinal Cord Injury by Promoting the Phagocytosis of Macrophages to Clean Myelin Debris. Front Cell Dev Biol 9: 772205.
11. Wu LL, et al. (2020). Repairing and Analgesic Effects of Umbilical Cord Mesenchymal Stem Cell Transplantation in Mice with Spinal Cord Injury. Biomed Res Int 2020: 7650354.
12. Yamazaki K, et al. (2021). Mesenchymal Stem Cell Sheet Promotes Functional Recovery and Palliates Neuropathic Pain in a Subacute Spinal Cord Injury Model. Stem Cells Int 2021: 9964877.

CHAPTER FIVE

Mesenchymal Stem Cells as Antimicrobial Agents

Talib Shareef, Tanveer Ahmad Mir and **Syed Nasir Ahmad**
Centre of Research for Development (CORD), University of Kashmir

Abstract

The exponential increase in microbial resistance in recent times has made it mandatory to look for safe and cost-effective alternatives to address the situation. Mesenchymal stem cells (MSC) have been documented to present strong antimicrobial features in both in-vitro and in-vivo settings. MSCs directly inhibit the growth of many high-priority pathogens, viz., Escherichia coli, Pseudomonas aeruginosa, S. aureus, Candida albicans and E. faecium, when stimulated with bacteria, IFNγ or even in certain cases without the presence of a particular stimulus. As far as the mechanistic prospects of the antimicrobial properties of MSCs are concerned a lot of the variables are yet to be explored, however it is established that there is involvement of a broad spectrum of biochemical and immunological processes, which are categorized into direct and indirect mechanisms. Former involves the secretion of AMPs, indoleamine 2,3 dioxygenase and interleukin (IL)-17 while as later includes the modulations in the host immune response against the pathogens. This chapter presents a brief account regarding the use of MSCs in tackling the crisis of AMR.

Keywords: Mesenchymal stem cells (MSCs), Antimicrobial resistance (AMR), Antimicrobial peptides (AMP)

Introduction

Antimicrobials, an unrivalled discovery in human history, rephrased the genre of medical sciences right from their inception. Being capable of specifically targeting microorganisms while inflicting no harm to people, earns them the moniker "magic bullets." Their discovery marked the start of the modern era of medicine, which opened a world of medical and surgical possibilities. Unfortunately, the extensive use of such wonderful medicines has led to the rapid emergence of antimicrobial drug resistance. As per the WHO reports, every year, 700,000 people worldwide die because of antimicrobial resistance (AMR), if current trends continue, drug-resistant illnesses might be responsible for 10 million fatalities per year as of 2050, and can be the reason for a catastrophic economic loss comparable to the 2008-2009 global financial crisis (World Health Organization, 2019). The resistance against antimicrobials has increased exponentially and with the advent of multidrug-resistant (MDR) and extensively drug-resistant (XDR) bacteria or "superbugs," AMR has evolved into a major concern that is constantly posing a severe threat to humankind. WHO and many other organizations like the Centres for Disease Control and Prevention (CDC), World Economic Forum have already declared antimicrobial resistance a global public health concern (Hoffman et al., 2015). A report, after scrutinizing the available bacterial genomes, deciphered the presence of over 20,000 potential resistant genes. The AMR or "Resistome" can thus be called a "covert pandemic", as it is responsible for huge morbidity and mortality globally and the return to post-antibiotic age cannot be excluded from being a possible scenario.

The fight against AMR is ongoing, and the development of new antibiotics are crucial. The facts and figures, taken together, raise a key question; is the era of antibiotics coming to an end? While antimicrobials have served mankind well over the last 70 years and more, microbes' ability to evolve promptly has made it necessary to focus on finding other solutions. The necessity of the hour is for a global and cumulative response involving all the above-mentioned plans, besides new ones, and the continual isolation of novel antimicrobial compounds from different sources. To address the situation of AMR, large-scale research in several aspects is being conducted, viz, resistance mechanisms are being explored further, alternatives to conventional antimicrobials are being explored like phage therapy, Lysins, CRISPR/ Cas 9 led technqiues, Bacteriocins, Antimicrobial peptide, Probiotics, Antibodies, etc (Fuente-Nunez et al., 2015; Lewis and Pamer et al., 2015). In recent past, MSCs due to their characteristic properties including their ability to modulate microbial growth is seen to have a role in preventing microbial infections and their resistance.

Antimicrobial properties of mesenchymal stem cells (MSCs)

The Mesenchymal stem cells present in living organisms exhibit strong antimicrobial activity through various mechanisms such as enhancing activity of phagocytes, modulate immune system, and secret various antimicrobial peptides (AMPs) and proteins that directly target the pathogens. It has been shown that MSCs have substantial role of bacterial elimination in case of sepsis, cystic fibrosis infections, and respiratory syndrome (Meisel et al., 2011).

Antimicrobial peptides also known as host defense peptides are the evolutionary conserved endogenous molecules that are found in all living organisms. They play an important role in first line defense mechanism against pathogenic microbes. Diverse forms of AMPs have been reported in nature, and their diversity can be ascribed to their broad-spectrum antimicrobial and immunomodulatory activity. Regardless of their heterogeneity, AMPs share some common characteristics. Most AMPs, for instance, are cationic in nature, and are positively charged (Farkas et al., 2017). They also possess an amphipathic structure having distinct hydrophilic and hydrophobic regions, with the positive charge playing a key role in the mechanism of action through electrostatic interaction between the target and the peptide.

The AMP molecules shows selective activity against various pathogens including viruses, bacteria, and fungi, and even cancer cells. Till date, several AMPs have been reported to express constitutively from MSCs including hepcidin, cathelicidin LL-37, lipocalin-2, and β-defensin-2 that can be modulated further during inflammation and infection. During bacterial infections increasing levels of hepcidin and LL-37 molecules have been reported in MSCs. The AMPs derived from the MSCs plays a key role in innate immune defence mechanism against various pathogens (Sung et al., 2016).

Unlike conventional antibiotics, AMPs interact with the cell membranes of bacteria via electrostatic interactions, thus makes difficult for bacteria to acquire resistance. Based on the mechanism of action AMPs are categorized into membrane acting peptides and non-membrane acting peptides. Membrane acting peptides mostly constitutes cationic peptides that causes disruption of membrane, whereas non-membrane peptides can enter inside the bacterial cytoplasm without destroying their outer membrane. Some AMPs, including LL-37 and defensin increase membrane permeability by forming transmembrane pores. While few AMPs such as hepcidin and pleurocidin enter inside bacterial cytoplasm and interferes with normal functioning of cell. Due to the presence of LPS or teichoic acid, the outer leaflet of prokaryotic cells is negatively charged. Cationic AMPs selectively bind with negatively charged outer microbial membranes, and achieve well-defined secondary structures, which results an increase in membrane permeability and eventually leads to disruption bacterial membranes (Sani & Separovic, 2016). AMPs also inhibit several processes like cell wall synthesis, nucleic acid synthesis, protein synthesis, and enzymatic activities. Due to intracellular inhibitory mechanisms antimicrobial peptides shows potent antibacterial activity. Therefore, AMPs can eliminate pathogens that are resistant to conventional antibiotics as MDR bacteria. These worthwhile features .make AMPs promising candidates for development of drugs.

Besides the antimicrobial activity of AMPs, MSCs also show other biological roles that can eliminate pathogenic infections (**Fig. 5.1**). In this regard, it has been demonstrated that AMPs secreted by epithelial cells displays various biological characteristics including anti-endotoxin and chemokine activities as well as bacterial opsonization, and protease inhibition. Particularly, β-defensins are chemotactic for mast cells, neutrophils, and macrophages. Similarly, cathelicidins are chemotactic for lymphocytes, neutrophils, and monocytes, and LL-37 neutralizes LPS of bacteria (Bals et al., 1999). Likewise, lipocalin-2 and hepcidin (Michels et al., 2015), they regulate iron availability that is important component for bacterial growth. The antimicrobial activity of mesenchymal stem cells provided by AMPs has been described for various sources of stem cells, despite different mechanism of action and antimicrobial range found in them. Most likely, these differences of MSCs in antimicrobial spectrum could be because of their explicit response to generate potent AMPs against specific class of pathogen challenge.

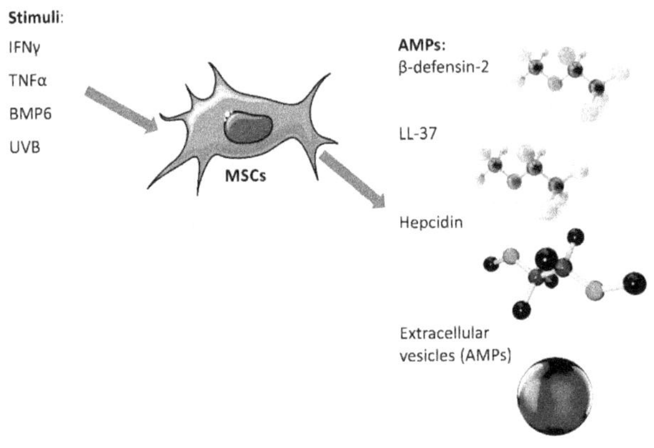

Fig. 5.1: A schematic representation showcasing the release of AMPs and extracellular vesicles by MSCs in response to the different stimuli. Viz., IFNγ, interferon gamma; TNFα, tumor necrosis factor alpha; BMP6, bone morphogenetic protein 6; UVB, ultraviolet B.

Antimicrobial resistance (AMR) is a serious concern that hampers the treatment of microbial infections, making many facets of modern antibiotics less efficient. The spike in the number of antimicrobial-resistant microbes is one of the most serious threats that society is confronting. Now researchers are finding other solutions to tackle the problem. Hence, developing novel antimicrobials or AMPs is best approach to address the scenario of antimicrobial drug resistance. Therefore, increasing the delivery of AMPs, their absorption, and bioavailability as well as synergy with antibiotics are some of the factors that can help to evade the infections. Therefore, it is imperative to focus on enhancing the features of MSCs through various genetic modification approaches, besides untangling the multi-target drug capacity of AMPs, must collaboratively lead to key approaches against pathogenic infections.

Role of MSCs in bacterial and viral infections

Worldwide, infectious disorders are a significant cause of mortality and morbidity. Pneumonia and respiratory infections are two of the most common fatal diseases. To treat infections and the ensuing organ and tissue damage brought on by infectious illnesses, newer therapeutic techniques must be developed due to the failure of widely used therapies, medications, and the increasing frequency of new infectious disease outbreaks. Non-hematopoietic cells known as mesenchymal stem cells (MSCs) can be found in bone marrow and a variety of other tissues, including adipose tissue, dental pulp, endometrium, the placenta, umbilical cord blood, synovial membrane, Wharton's jelly, and ocular tissues (Dominici et al. 2006). To isolate MSCs, tissues are physically or biochemically disintegrated, resulting in clusters of plastic adherent cells (Mushahary et al., 2018). Using flow cytometry sorting, MSCs may also be selected depending on the expression of their cell surface markers (Masterson et al., 2018; Gugjoo et al. 2020; Gugjoo, 2022).

MSCs have emerged as a viable therapy option for viruses-related illnesses such as immunologic abnormalities in HIV, chronic hepatitis in HBV, and acute lung injury in influenza virus. Since MSCs express receptors and coreceptors for the entrance of various kinds of viruses, administering MSCs to patients who are virus-infected might reduce their therapeutic effectiveness. Additionally, it has been noted that immunocompromised people are more likely to have viral reactivation. Numerous herpesviruses have been found to be capable of infecting MSCs, which thereafter lose their ability to function (Maytawan et al. 2015). The antimicrobial effector role of MSCs was investigated to further assess the therapeutic effects of these cells in transplant patients. MSCs are intriguing therapeutic tools for the treatment of immune-mediated disorders, including Graft versus host disease, a condition associated with a high risk of infection. The antimicrobial peptide human cathelicidin hCAP-18/LL-37, which aids in bacterial clearance both in vitro and in vivo, was remarkably produced and secreted in large amounts by MSCs (Krasnodembskaya et al., 2010).

Mesenchymal stem cells (MSCs) have the capacity to suppress bacterial infections. MSCs‘ antimicrobial effect relies on both direct and indirect mechanisms since they release paracrine substances that may hinder bacterial growth or increase immune cells' phagocytic activity. With more than a million fatalities each year worldwide, tuberculosis is still a life-threatening illness. The severe inflammatory response caused by tuberculosis leads to the development of granulomas, which are structured cellular aggregations that surround mycobacterial cells. In addition to the various immune cells that produce granulomas, such as macrophages that form foaming cells and migrated lymphocytes that subsequently arrive at the site of infection, several studies have discovered that bone marrow derived MSCs stem cells cover the outer surface of the granulomas therefore provide desirable niche that contains persistent mycobacteria and maintain the infection in balance (Garhyan et al., 2015). In an in vitro experiment, it was shown that MSCs produced from bone marrow could stop *Staphylococcus aureus* from growing when the bacteria were injected to synovial fluid (Yagi et al., 2020). The influence of soluble products of MSCs from various donor sites, including bone marrow or adipose tissue, on cystic fibrosis infection, has been confirmed by a separate investigation. In an in vivo mice model the experiment showed that soluble products of MSCs could reduce colony-forming units (CFUs) of *Staphylococcus aureus, Streptococcus pneumonia* and *Pseudomonas aeruginosa.* Additionally, this activity has raised the infection's susceptibility to antibiotic treatment (Sutton et al., 2016).

Conclusion

The calibre of MSCs to be used as an alternative to or in combination with the conventional mode of antibiotic therapy is enormous. MSCs present some incredible features over conventional medicaments, viz., sensing and migration to the infection site, acting as bioactive pumps and thus continuously releasing AMPs at the infection site, and specifically releasing the desired AMPs based on the stimulus and requirement. Moreover, the extracellular vesicles (EV) produced by the MSCs have been shown to be possessing a huge potential. These vesicles present anti-bacterial, anti-apoptotic, wound-healing and even anti-tumor activities. MSCs are indeed the potential candidates to curb the crisis of AMR, nevertheless a lot of further research needs to be carried out in exploring the paradigm of stimulus and AMP production, economical parameters like shelf-life and cost, and the involvement of genetic modifications that will enhance the MSC features. Furthermore, the role of MSCs in cases of bacterial infections has been studied in great detail; however, considering the potential of these cells, the world of fungi and viruses is highly unexplored yet.

References

1. Bals R, et al. (1999). Augmentation of innate host defense by expression of a cathelicidin antimicrobial peptide. Infect Immun 67: 60849.
2. Dominici M, et al. (2006). Minimal criteria for defining multipotent mesenchymal stromal cells. The International Society for Cellular

Therapy position statement. Cytotherapy8: 315–317

3. Farkas A, et al. (2017). Comparative analysis of the bacterial membrane disruption effect of two natural plant antimicrobial peptides. Front Microbiol 8: 1–12.
4. Fuente-Nunez de la C, & Lu TK. (2017). CRISPR-Cas9 technology: applications in genome engineering, development of sequence-specific antimicrobials, and prospects. Integr Biol (Camb.) 9: 109–122.
5. Garhyan J, et al. (2015). Preclinical and Clinical Evidence of Mycobacterium tuberculosis Persistence in the Hypoxic Niche of Bone Marrow Mesenchymal Stem Cells after Therapy. Am J Pathol 185: 1924-1934.
6. Gugjoo MB. (2022). Therapeutic Applications of Mesenchymal Stem Cells in Veterinary Medicine. Springer Nature. pp. 341-374.
7. Gugjoo MB, & Pal Amar. (2020). Mesenchymal stem cells in Veterinary Sciences. Springer Nature. PP. 1-337.
8. Hoffman SJ, et al. (2015). Strategies for achieving global collective action on antimicrobial resistance. Bull World Health Organ 93(12): 867–876.
9. Krasnodembskaya A, et al. (2010). "Antibacterial effect of human mesenchymal stem cells is mediated in part from secretion of the antimicrobial peptide LL-37," Stem Cells 28(12): 2229–2238.
10. Lewis BB, & Pamer EG. (2017). Microbiota therapy for Clostridium difficile and antibiotic resistant enteric infections. Ann Rev Microbiol 71: 157–178.
11. Masterson C, et al. (2018). Syndecan-2-positive, Bone Marrow-derived Human Mesenchymal Stromal Cells Attenuate Bacterial-induced Acute Lung Injury and Enhance Resolution of Ventilator-induced Lung Injury in Rats. Anesthesiol129: 502–516.
12. Maytawan T, et al. (2015). "Mesenchymal Stromal Cells and Viral Infection", Stem Cells International, vol. 2015, Article ID 860950, 8 pages.
13. Meisel R, et al. (2011). Human but not murine multipotent mesenchymal stromal cells exhibit broad-spectrum antimicrobial effector function mediated by indoleamine 2, 3-dioxygenase. Leukemia 25: 648–54.
14. Michels K, et al. (2015) Hepcidin and host defense against infectious diseases. PLoS Pathog 11: e1004998.
15. Mushahary D, et al. (2018). Isolation, cultivation, and characterization of human mesenchymal stem cells. Cytometry A 93: 19–31.

16. Sani MA, & Separovic F. (2016). How membrane-active peptides get into lipid membranes. Acc Chem Res 49(6): 1130-1138.
17. Sung DK, et al. (2016). Antibacterial effect of mesenchymal stem cells against Escherichia coli is mediated by secretion of beta-defensin-2 via toll-like receptor 4 signalling. Cell Microbiol 18: 424–36.
18. Sutton MT, et al. (2016). Antimicrobial Properties of Mesenchymal Stem Cells: Therapeutic Potential for Cystic Fibrosis Infection, and Treatment. Stem Cells Int 2016: Article ID: 5303048.
19. World Health Organization. (2019). Report released on 29 April, available on https:// www.who.int/news/item/29-04-2019-new-report-calls-for-urgent-action-to-avert antimicrobial-resistance-crisis, accessed on 4. 12. 2022
20. Yagi H, et al. (2020). Antimicrobial Activity of Mesenchymal Stem Cells against Staphylococcus aureus. Stem Cell Res Therapy 11: Article No. 293.

CHAPTER SIX

Mesenchymal Stem Cell for Hepatic Fibrosis

Amitha Banu S[1], Manjusha K M[1], Sharun Khan[1], Mudasir B Gugjoo[2], Abhijit M Pawde[1] and Amarpal[1]

[1]*Division of Surgery, ICAR-IVRI, Izatnagar, Bareilly, UP, India*

[2]*Veterinary Clinical Complex, FVSc & AH, SKUAST-K, Shuhama, Srinagar, J&K, India*

Abstract

Liver fibrosis is one of the most common sequelae of chronic liver diseases. The end stage of liver fibrosis is liver cirrhosis, for which the ultimate effective treatment strategy is liver transplantation. But liver transplantation is neither economically feasible nor easily accessible. This necessitates the need for alternative therapy. Mesenchymal stem cells (MSCs)-based therapy has been suggested to be a breakthrough for treating liver fibrosis based on preclinical and clinical studies. Even though the exact mechanism of MSCs in liver fibrosis is not fully elucidated, it is proposed that the ability to differentiate into hepatocytes, immunomodulatory function, and paracrine action is the underlying mechanism through which MSCs exhibit their therapeutic action in liver fibrosis. This chapter discusses the advantages, mechanisms, and clinical applications of MSCs in treating hepatic fibrosis.

Keywords: Liver fibrosis, Hepatic fibrosis, Mesenchymal stem cells, Hepatocytes, Stem cell therapy

Introduction

The liver is the body's largest gland performing various major functions like the metabolism of nutrients, scavenging toxins, participating in protein synthesis and glycogen storage, etc. The major functional cells within the liver are called hepatocytes. The liver is much more prone to injuries as it is in direct contact with external toxins (Zhang & Wang, 2013). Following any injury, the liver is subjected to various functional disorders like cirrhosis, hepatitis, and hepatocellular carcinoma. The fibrotic and inflammatory condition of the liver caused by chronic liver injury is called liver fibrosis (Cao et al., 2020). The major etiological agents responsible for hepatic fibrosis include viral hepatitis infections, alcoholism, fatty liver diseases, and autoimmune hepatitis. Liver fibrosis is a worldwide health concern due to its increased morbidity and mortality in developed and undeveloped countries.

The disease is characterized by the loss of functional liver cells and the replacement of normal tissue with fibrous tissue. During liver fibrosis, there will be enhanced extracellular matrix accumulation with abundant collagen II and III. This deposition leads to scar formation, and their common sequelae is the formation of hepatic cirrhosis (Feng et al., 2019). Even though various treatment strategies exist for hepatic fibrosis, none are fully effective except for liver transplantation (**Fig. 6.1**). Liver transplantation is considered to be the golden standard for the treatment of hepatic cirrhosis. Still, the shortage of donors and organs and the cost and necessities for lifelong immunosuppressive drugs limits their use. In such a scenario, an alternative treatment using stem cells is suggested to be an effective alternative (Zhu et al., 2021).

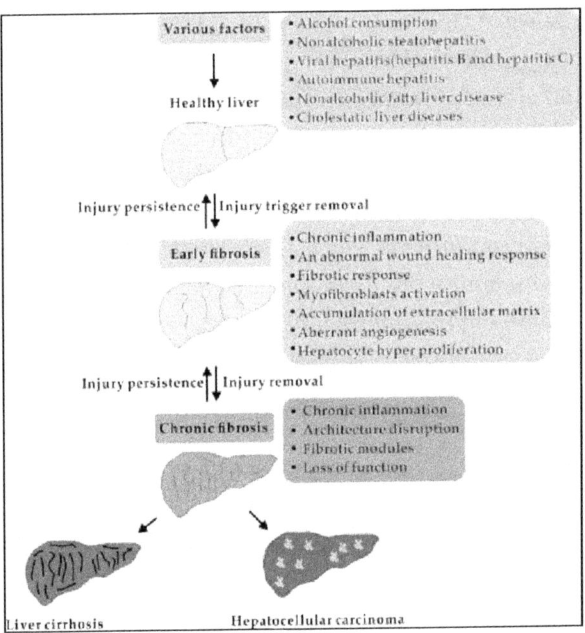

Fig. 5.1: Pathogenesis of Liver cirrhosis. Reproduced from He et al., (2020) under the Creative Commons Attribution (CC BY) license (http://creativecommons.org/licenses/by/4.0/).

Mesenchymal stem cells (MSCs) are multipotent stromal cells with self-renewing capacity and multilineage differentiation. The ability to differentiate into hepatocytes and their immunomodulatory properties pave the way for using MSCs in treating hepatic fibrosis (Volarevic et al., 2014). Various studies suggest that the presence of growth factors, cytokines, chemical compounds, hepatocytes, etc., present within the MSCs helps them differentiate into hepatocytes. Human MSCs isolated from different sources like bone marrow, adipose tissue, amniotic fluid, umbilical cord, dental pulp, and fetal pulp have the potential to differentiate into hepatocytes. Under the influence of hepatocyte growth factor (HGF) and basic fibroblast growth factor (bFGF), there is controlled differentiation of rat MSCs into hepatocytes (Shu et al., 2004). For hepatic differentiation, MSCs are finally treated with differentiation media (culture media supplemented with HGF, bFGF, and nicotinamide) for a week, and it is followed by treatment with maturation medium (culture medium containing dexamethasone, insulin, transferring, etc) (Lee et al., 2004; Gugjoo, 2022).

Studies demonstrating MSCs potential therapeutic action

Systemic administration of MSCs decreases chemical-induced liver injuries in the murine liver failure model. Intravenous injection of MSCs successfully engraft at the damaged site, reduce inflammation and enhance lymphocyte proliferation. In addition, the administration of MSCs reduce various pro-inflammatory cytokines in the liver and serum (Zhu et al., 2013). Literature also suggests the immunomodulatory capacity of conditioned media derived from the human BM-MSCs in an experimental liver injury model (Xagorari et al., 2013). This is possibly attributed to soluble factors like IL-6, VEGF, HGF, and IGF binding proteins contained in the MSC-conditioned media (Jang et al., 2014). The therapeutic applications of MSCs in liver cirrhosis are well documented in experiemntal and clinical studies. The therapeutic effect of MSCs in liver fibrosis is mainly attributed to the secretome containing tropic and immunomodulatory factors released by the MSCs. These factors are responsible for altering the function of hepatic stellate cells, where activation of hepatic stellate cells is a major event in developing hepatic fibrosis (Parekkadan et al., 2007). In addition to reducing the proliferation of stellate cells, MSCs are responsible for reducing collagen type I synthesis and promoting apoptosis of hepatic stellate cells through the secretion of HGF and Nerve growth factors (Lin et al., 2009). Moreover, MSCs produce an antifibrotic effect in the cirrhotic liver by enhancing the expression of matrix metalloproteinase (MMP 9), which is found to have a role in the degradation of extracellular matrix. MSCs may also improve the local microenvironment by up-regulating gene expression of VEG, HGF, IL-10, and MMP 9, thereby promoting liver regeneration (Higashiyama et al.,2007).

The potential mechanism of MSCs in liver fibrosis is through the migration of cells in the liver, hepatogenic differentiation, paracrine mechanism, autophagy, and immunoregulation (Zhu et al.,2021). MSCs are found to have the potential to differentiate into hepatocyte-like cells and are a promising source of liver regeneration. However, they can effectively differentiate into myofibroblast but not into all liver cells, thereby limiting their application. The addition of growth factors like HGF, bFGF, etc., is shown to potentiate liver differentiation. Both AD-MSCs and BM-MSCs are shown to have effective hepatocyte differentiation and promote liver function integration (Aurich et al., 2009). Moreover, engineered cell aggregates can also promote differentiation and helps in the treatment of liver fibrosis. Another potential mechanism of MSCs is attributed to their paracrine effect (Cao et al., 2019). Due to their paracrine action, MSCs release extracellular vesicles and other soluble molecules into their immediate microenvironment. These secretory factors are also present in the media in which MSCs are harvested, known as conditioned media. MSCs and MSC-CM have thereby shown effective potential for treating chronic liver fibrosis. In addition to these paracrine factors, other factors such as cytokines, growth factors, and chemokines exhibit anti-inflammatory properties and angiogenesis-induced apoptosis and help in hepatic repair (**Fig. 6.2**) (Skalnikova, 2013).

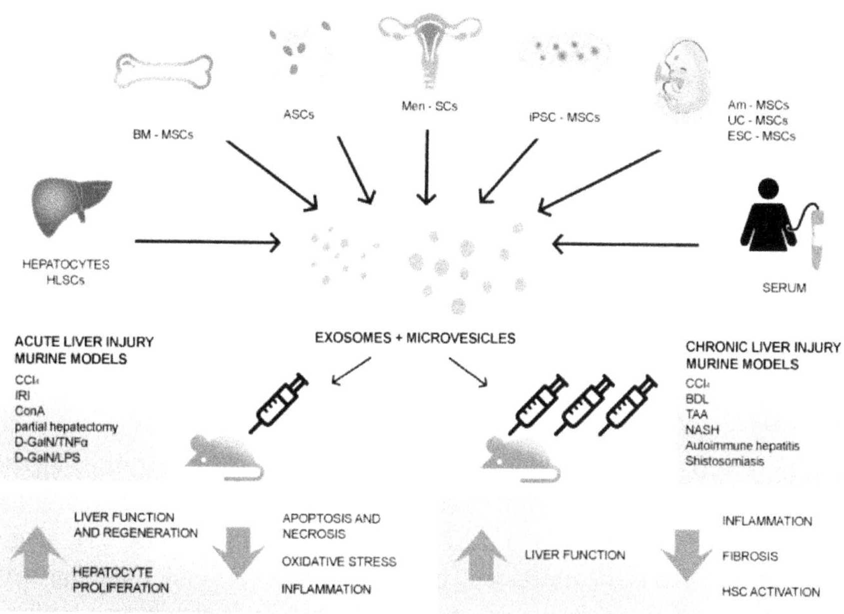

Fig. 5.2: Exosome in hepatic fibrosis. Reproduced from Bruno et al. (2020) under the Creative Commons Attribution (CC BY) license (http://creativecommons.org/licenses/by/4.0/).

MSCs exert immunosuppressive potential, which also helps in the therapeutic effects of MSCs in liver regeneration. However, the exact mechanism of tissue protection and immunomodulation of MSCs is still unclear. It is attributed to the interaction of various immune cells (activated by MSCs paracrine secretions), such as macrophages, neutrophils, myeloid-derived suppressor cells, etc. MSCs inherently lack the MHC II receptor, which is responsible for the naïve immunoevasive effect exerted by them (Mun et al., 2018). Another important mechanism through which MSCs counteract liver fibrosis is autophagy. Autophagy is the cell degradation mechanism by employing lysosomes to destroy damaged organelles and macromolecules. It helps reduce inflammation, apoptosis, and oxidative stress in diseased cells and thereby paves the way for the therapeutic roles of MSCs. Furthermore, autophagy helps in reducing hypoxia tolerance in aging MSCs, regulates immunomodulatory functions, and enhances antifibrotic effects (Parzych & Klionsky, 2014). The combined action of all these mechanisms contributes to the successful management of liver fibrosis and prevents end-stage hepatic cirrhosis; therefore, MSCs are a promising tool in the therapeutic potential of liver fibrosis.

The *in vivo* studies have established the therapeutic role of MSCs in various animal liver fibrosis models. Most MSCs are derived from the bone marrow of mice (Berardis et al., 2015). Several *in vivo* studies have revealed the efficiency of stem cells to differentiate into hepatocyte-like cells and alleviate liver fibrosis in experimental animal models. Mouse embryonic stem cells administered into the induced hepatic fibrosis models show hepatic differentiation of stem cells that incorporated well with the liver parenchyma. A significant reduction in the severity of liver fibrosis without any evidence of tumorigenicity is also seen (Moriya et al., 2007; Moriya et al., 2008).

The effect of mesenchymal stem cells on the carbon tetrachloride-induced liver fibrosis model in mice is also studied (Liu et al., 2015). It has been demonstrated that MSCs can attenuate liver damage in the early stages in mice, and the key component involved is vascular endothelial growth factor (VEGF). In addition, the therapeutic potential of human umbilical cord-derived mesenchymal stem cells (hUC-MSCs) on acute-on-chronic liver failure (ACLF) and acute-on-chronic liver injury (ACLI) in rats has also been investigated (He et al., 2021). It has been concluded that the transplantation of MSCs could improve the degree of fibrosis, liver function, and liver damage and promote liver repair in rats with ACLI and ACLF by reversing the imbalance of the Stat1/Stat3 pathway and inhibiting the notch signaling. A similar study investigated the functional role of bone marrow-derived mesenchymal stem cells (BM-MSCs) in treating liver fibrosis in a mouse model by targeting intrahepatic macrophage subsets (Li et al., 2021). BM-MSCs play a pivotal role in ameliorating hepatic fibrosis by secreting antifibrogenic cytokines and inducing apoptosis through $Ly6C^{hi}/Ly6C^{lo}$ macrophage switch. Apart from lab animals, large animal experimental studies (acute and chronic hepatic injury models) too show autologous or allogeneic AD-MSCs (Matsuda et al. 2017; Teshima et al. 2017) or BM-MSCs (Nishimura et al. 2019) of variable doses improve the hepatic injury. The clinical improvement in the form of improved liver function tests is reported.

Clinical trials

Irrespective of the various therapies developed and investigated, the treatment of liver cirrhosis remains challenging. Various studies have proven that MSCs therapy benefits liver cirrhotic patients. The route, dosage, and frequency of cell administration and the stage of liver fibrosis are important factors for therapeutic considerations. Stem cell therapy has proved to be a promising tool for liver diseases through its immunoregulatory and anti-apoptotic mechanisms (Berardis et al., 2015). The MSCs used for clinical trials are mainly derived from adipose tissue, bone marrow, amniotic membrane, menstrual blood, umbilical fluid, etc. The limitations of BM-MSCs are their lacunae concerning vitality and aging differentiation, whereas AD-MSCs are associated with difficulty in isolation (Jang et al., 2014). In a study involving 56 patients with hepatitis virus-related fibrosis, MSCs treatment was more effective than control by increasing the factors responsible for liver regeneration, such as TREG-related transcription factors. It also increased serum TGF levels and reduced serum IL-17, TNF-A, and IL-6 in such patients (Mohamadnejad et al., 2013). Similar results were also obtained by other study (Fang et al., 2018). It was also reported that MSCs reduced jaundice-like syndrome and reduced the serum levels of aminotransferase and bilirubin in such patients.

Apart from this, MSCs transplantation has been successfully applied in patients suffering from alcoholic cirrhosis, autoimmune liver cirrhosis, and hepatolenticular degeneration. In such cases, MSCs improved histological analysis course and decreased the levels of pro-inflammatory mediators. In addition, MSCs transplantation also reduces collagen deposition and helps prevent fibrosis. In liver cirrhosis, MSCs are also found to increase the serum levels of albumin but have not influenced the level of coagulation indicators. One of the studies reports that combining MSCs and traditional supportive therapy in liver cirrhosis patients improves the quality of life and clinical symptoms (Sang et al. 2018). Further studies are required to better understand the safety and effects of MSCs transplantation in clinical settings.

Human umbilical cord-derived mesenchymal stem cells (hUC-MSCs) have been used for clinical potential due to their low immunogenicity, high proliferation potential, and rich growth factors (Kim et al., 2018). The hUC-MSCs have positive therapeutic potential for acute liver failure and liver cirrhosis (He et al., 2021). hUC-MSCs could repair damaged liver tissues by inhibiting hepatocyte apoptosis and promoting hepatocyte regeneration (Yu et al., 2016). MSCs therapy, when applied at the compensatory stage of liver cirrhosis, was found to have an outstanding therapeutic effect (Zhang et al., 2020). In addition, autologous mesenchymal stem cell therapy improved liver function and histologic fibrosis in alcoholic patients (Jang et al., 2014).

Cell-free therapy for hepatic fibrosis

MSC generally differentiate into hepatic-like cells and exhibit antifibrotic potential *in-vivo* with some immunomodulatory potential. But there is every chance the transplantation may result in uncontrolled adverse effects, including tumorigenic potential and cell rejection (Nazarie et al., 2021). MSCs exert its anti-inflammatory effect chiefly through its paracrine activity, releasing soluble factors into its immediate environment. These soluble factors are predominantly extracellular vesicles carrying an adequate amount of signal molecules like proteins, mRNA, miRNA, etc. Currently, researchers have shifted their interest towards a novel alternative to MSCs. Cell-free therapy using these extracellular vesicles has gained popularity and is a novel alternative for MSCs in many disease conditions (Rani et al., 2015). The paracrine effect of MSC on the regenerative mechanism of hepatic fibrosis has already been discussed. It paves the way for the extracellular vesicles to be a useful alternative in treating hepatic fibrosis. According to recent research, exosomes serve as a conduit for intercellular communication, delivering necessary factors for the resolution of liver fibrosis. Evidence suggests that exosomes and EV can inhibit the activation of macrophages and cytokine secretions. In addition to this, EV has the potential to control extracellular matrix production and decrease the formation of fibrotic scars. There is much evidence that EV can also allay the activation of hepatic stellate cells, which are otherwise actively involved in the formation of the myofibroblast (Chen et al., 2019).

Mice model of induced hepatic fibrosis that used conditioned media-MSC injection reported decreased levels of hepatic enzymes and collagen deposition in the liver (Pinheiro et al. 2021). Another CCl4-induced liver fibrosis model study shows that post injection of CM from BM-MSCs leads to anti-inflammatory response (Yin et al., 2021). Thus, CM from MSCs plays a major role in the repair of the liver and inhibits inflammatory infiltration, and promotes apoptosis.

MSC-EVs suppress fibrotic marker expression (Li et al., 2013, Jun et al., 2020). EVs from the human umbilical cord-MSCs inhibited the activation of hepatic stem cells *in vitro* by reducing the expression of inflammatory mediators (Fiore et al., 2020). An *in vivo* study of liver fibrosis-induced mice models yielded similar results, with significant downregulation of the expression of fibrotic markers (Zhang et al., 2021). Exosomes derived from BM-MSCs reduce inflammation by suppressing the infiltration of inflammatory cells (Jiang et al., 2018) and reducing pro-inflammatory cytokines (Qu et al., 2017, Ohara et al., 2018). The expression of inflammatory cytokines was found to be reduced in Kupffer cells after treatment with EVs isolated from Amnion-derived MSCs (Ohara et al., 2018).

Antifibrotic efficacy of adipose-derived extracellular nanovesicles (AD-ENVs) is also evaluated in rat liver fibrosis models. Systemic administration of AD-ENVs resulted in increased accumulation of fibrotic liver tissue and restoration of liver functionality in liver fibrosis models by significantly reducing hepatic enzymes and collagen deposition. This study has shown that AD-ENVs demonstrate a potential candidate for the therapeutic management of liver fibrosis and other chronic liver diseases (Han et al., 2020). In one study, engineered MSC-EVs were evaluated as potential therapeutics for liver fibrosis by hydrophobic insertion of a vitamin A as the activated HSC-targeting moiety. These engineered EVs were administered systemically in induced hepatic fibrosis mouse models, and V-EVs were found to accumulate in fibrotic liver tissue. Upon uptake by hepatic stellate cells, V-EVs reversed the activation of stellate cells. V-EVs modulated the fibrotic cascade, enhancing therapeutic efficacy for liver fibrosis (You et al., 2021).

MSC therapy in liver-risk or benefit

The dilemma regarding the therapeutic application of MSCs for liver diseases still exists despite its beneficial effects. The drawbacks are mainly concerned with its fibrogenic potential and untoward differentiation into myofibroblasts. These undesirable effects mainly occur due to improper routes of administration or depend on the time frame. The available evidence indicates that BM-MSCs, when administered intravenously, will rarely differentiate into hepatocytes in acute liver injury. In addition, there is increased differentiation into myofibroblasts in the acute liver injury model. MSCs enhance fibrogenic potential when administrated at the liver injury phase, whereas it promotes healing when administered at the liver resolution phase. This indicates the importance of the time frame of MSC therapy in liver diseases (Volarevic et al., 2014). Another concern regarding the use of MSCs in liver disease is the immune rejection of transplanted cells. It is well known that allogeneic stem cells have more practical therapeutic value. But allogenic stem cells show poor engraftment in the liver compared with autogenous stem cells (Mohamadnejad et al., 2013). In addition, some concerns regarding the malignant transformation of MSCs limit their use. Although the malignant transformation of MSCs is rarely reported in clinical trials, there is every chance for tumor occurrence in a longer span.

Conclusion

The hepatogenic potential, immunomodulatory properties, and paracrine action of the MSCs indicate their use in hepatic fibrosis compared with conventional therapy. Furthermore, antifibrotic and antioxidant properties also contribute to the beneficial effect of treating liver fibrosis using MSCs. However, concerns regarding the clinical use of MSCs for liver fibrosis, like optimum time, delivery route, etc., need to be addressed. Moreover, controlled clinical studies with long-term follow-ups are required to implement MSC therapy for liver fibrosis in clinical settings.

References

1. Aurich H, et al. (2009). Hepatocyte differentiation of mesenchymal stem cells from human adipose tissue in vitro promotes hepatic integration in vivo. Gut 58(4): 570-581.
2. Berardis S, et al. (2015). Use of mesenchymal stem cells to treat liver fibrosis: current situation and future prospects. World J Gastroenterol 21(3): 742.
3. Bruno S, et al. (2020). Extracellular vesicles: a therapeutic option for liver fibrosis. Int J Mol Sci 21(12): 4255.
4. Cao L, et al. (2019). Construction of multicellular aggregate by E-cadherin coated microparticles enhancing the hepatic specific differentiation of mesenchymal stem cells. Acta Biomaterialia95: 382-394.
5. Cao Y, et al. (2020). Mesenchymal stem cell therapy for liver fibrosis/cirrhosis. Ann Transl Med 8(8): 562.
6. Chen L, et al. (2017). Human Menstrual Blood-Derived Stem Cells Ameliorate Liver Fibrosis in Mice by Targeting Hepatic Stellate Cells via Paracrine Mediators. Stem Cells Transl Med 6: 272-84.
7. Chen L, et al. (2019). Combatting fibrosis: exosome-based therapies in the regression of liver fibrosis. Hepatol Commun 3(2): 180-192.
8. Feng J, et al. (2019). Procyanidin B2 inhibits the activation of hepatic stellate cells and angiogenesis via the Hedgehog pathway during liver fibrosis. J Cell Mol Med 23(9): 6479-6493.

9. Fiore E, et al. (2020). Human umbilical cord perivascular cells-derived extracellular vesicles mediate the transfer of IGF-I to the liver and ameliorate hepatic fibrogenesis in mice. Gene Therapy 27(1): 62-73.
10. Han HS, et al. (2020). Human adipose stem cell-derived extracellular nanovesicles for treatment of chronic liver fibrosis. J Controll Release 320: 328-336.
11. He Y, et al. (2021). Human umbilical cord-derived mesenchymal stem cells improve the function of liver in rats with acute-on-chronic liver failure via downregulating Notch and Stat1/Stat3 signaling. Stem Cell Res Therapy 12(1): 1-19.
12. He Z, et al. (2020). The Roles and Mechanisms of lncRNAs in Liver Fibrosis. International J Mol Sci 21(4): 1482.
13. Higashiyama R, et al. (2007). Bone marrow–derived cells express matrix metalloproteinases and contribute to regression of liver fibrosis in mice. Hepatol 45(1): 213-222.
14. Gugjoo MB. (2022). Mesenchymal Stem Cells Therapeutic Applications in Gastrointestinal Disorders. In: Therapeutic Applications of Mesenchymal stem cells in Veterinary medicine. Springer. pp. 247-278.
15. Jang YO, et al. (2014). Histological improvement following administration of autologous bone marrow-derived mesenchymal stem cells for alcoholic cirrhosis: a pilot study. Liver Int 34: 33-41.
16. Jang YO, et al. (2014). Histological improvement following administration of autologous bone marrow-derived mesenchymal stem cells for alcoholic cirrhosis: a pilot study. Liver Int 34(1): 33-41.
17. Jiang W, et al. (2018). Human umbilical cord MSC-derived exosomes suppress the development of CCl4-induced liver injury through antioxidant effect. Stem cells Int 2018: 6079642.
18. Jun JH, et al. (2020). Exosomes from placenta-derived mesenchymal stem cells are involved in liver regeneration in hepatic failure induced by bile duct ligation. Stem cells International, 2020: 5485738.
19. Kim JH, et al (2018). Comparison of immunological characteristics of mesenchymal stem cells from the periodontal ligament, umbilical cord, and adipose tissue. Stem Cells Int 2018: 8429042.
20. Li T, et al. (2013). Exosomes derived from human umbilical cord mesenchymal stem cells alleviate liver fibrosis. Stem cells Dev 22(6): 845-854.
21. Lin N, et al. (2009). Nerve growth factor-mediated paracrine regulation of hepatic stellate cells by multipotent mesenchymal stromal cells. Life

Sci 85(7-8): 291-295.

22. Matsuda T, et al. (2017). A Canine Liver Fibrosis Model to Develop a Therapy for Liver Cirrhosis Using Cultured Bone Marrow–Derived Cells. Hepatol Commun 1(7), 691-703.
23. Mohamadnejad M, et al. (2013). Randomized placebo-controlled trial of mesenchymal stem cell transplantation in decompensated cirrhosis. Liver Int 33(10): 1490-1496.
24. Moriya K, et al. (2008). Embryonic stem cells reduce liver fibrosis in CCl4-treated mice. Int J Exp Pathol 89(6): 401-409.
25. Moriya K, et al. (2007). Embryonic stem cells develop into hepatocytes after intrasplenic transplantation in CCl4-treated mice. World J Gastroenterol 13(6): 866.
26. Mun CH, et al. (2018). The expression of immunomodulation-related cytokines and genes of adipose-and bone marrow-derived human mesenchymal stromal cells from early to late passages. Tissue Eng Reg Med 15(6): 771-779.
27. Nazarie (Ignat) S-R, et al. (2021). Regenerative Potential of Mesenchymal Stem Cells' (MSCs) Secretome for Liver Fibrosis Therapies. Int J Mol Sci 22(24): 13292.
28. Nishimura T, et al. (2019). Liver regeneration therapy through the hepatic artery-infusion of cultured bone marrow cells in a canine liver fibrosis model. PLoS ONE 14(1): e0210588.
29. Ohara M, et al. (2018). Extracellular vesicles from amnion-derived mesenchymal stem cells ameliorate hepatic inflammation and fibrosis in rats. Stem cells international, 2018: 3212643.
30. Parekkadan B, et al. (2007). Immunomodulation of activated hepatic stellate cells by mesenchymal stem cells. Biochem Biophys Res Commun 363(2): 247-252.
31. Parzych KR, & Klionsky DJ. (2014). An overview of autophagy: morphology, mechanism, and regulation. Antioxidants Redox Sign 20(3): 460-473.
32. Pinheiro D, et al. (2021). Effects of mesenchymal stem cells conditioned medium treatment in mice with cholestatic liver fibrosis. Life Sci 281: 119768.
33. Qu Y, et al. (2017). Exosomes derived from miR-181-5p-modified adipose-derived mesenchymal stem cells prevent liver fibrosis via autophagy activation. J Cell Mol Med 21(10): 2491-2502.

34. Rani S, et al. (2015). Mesenchymal stem cell-derived extracellular vesicles: toward cell-free therapeutic applications. Mol Therapy 23(5): 812-823.
35. Sang W, et al. (2018). Therapeutic efficacy and safety of umbilical cord mesenchymal stem cell transplantation for liver cirrhosis in Chinese population: a meta-analysis. Clin Res Hepatol Gastroenterol 42(3): 193-204.
36. Shi MX, et al. (2005). Flk1+ mesenchymal stem cells ameliorate carbon tetrachloride-induced liver fibrosis in mice. Sheng wu gong cheng xue bao= Chin J Biotechnol 21(3): 396-401.
37. Shu SN, et al. (2004). Hepatic differentiation capability of rat bone marrow-derived mesenchymal stem cells and hematopoietic stem cells. World J Gastroenterol 10(19): 2818.
38. Skalnikova HK. (2013). Proteomic techniques for characterisation of mesenchymal stem cell secretome. Biochimie 95(12): 2196-2211.
39. Teshima T, et al (2017). Allogenic Adipose Tissue-Derived Mesenchymal Stem Cells Ameliorate Acute Hepatic Injury in Dogs. Stem Cells Int 2017: 3892514.
40. Volarevic V, et al. (2014). Concise review: therapeutic potential of mesenchymal stem cells for the treatment of acute liver failure and cirrhosis. Stem Cells 32(11): 2818-2823.
41. Xagorari A, et al. (2013). Protective effect of mesenchymal stem cell-conditioned medium on hepatic cell apoptosis after acute liver injury. Int J Clin Exp Pathol 6(5): 831.
42. Yin F, et al. (2021). Effect of Hepatocyte Growth Factor-Transfected Human Umbilical Cord Mesenchymal Stem Cells on Hepatic Stellate Cells by Regulating Transforming Growth Factor-β1/Smads Signaling Pathway. Stem Cells Dev 30(21): 1070-1081.
43. You DG, et al. (2021). Vitamin A-coupled stem cell-derived extracellular vesicles regulate the fibrotic cascade by targeting activated hepatic stellate cells in vivo. J Contrl Release 336: 285-295.
44. Yu SJ, et al. (2016). Safety and efficacy of human umbilical cord derived-mesenchymal stem cell transplantation for treating patients with HBV-related decompensated cirrhosis. Zhonghua Gan Zang Bing Za Zhi. 24(1): 51–5.
45. Zhang P, et al. (2021). Exosomes from microRNA-145-5p-modified HUCB-MSCs attenuate CCl4-induced hepatic fibrosis via down-regulating FSCN1 expression. Life Sci 2021: 119404.

46. Zhang S, et al. (2020). The clinical application of mesenchymal stem cells in liver disease: the current situation and potential future. Annals Transl Med 8(8): 565.
47. Zhang Z, & Wang FS. (2013). Stem cell therapies for liver failure and cirrhosis. J Hepatol 59(1): 183-185.
48. Zhu M, et al. (2021). Applications of mesenchymal stem cells in liver fibrosis: novel strategies, mechanisms, and clinical practice. Stem Cells Int 2021: 6546780.
49. Zhu X, et al. (2013). Effects of transplanted bone-marrow-derived mesenchymal stem cells in animal models of acute hepatitis. Cell Tissue Res 351(3): 477-486.

CHAPTER SEVEN

Mesenchymal Stem Cells for Osteoarthritis

Sharun Khan[1], Manjusha K M[1], Amitha Banu S[1], Manish Arya[1], Auqib Hamid[2], Shakir A Rather[2], □Mudasir B Gugjoo[3], Abhijit M Pawde[1]and Amarpal[1]

[1]Division of Surgery, ICAR-IVRI, Izatnagar, Bareilly, UP, India

[2]Veterinary Surgery & Radiology, [3]Veterinary Clinical Complex, FVSc & AH, SKUAST-K, Shuhama, Srinagar, J&K, India

Abstract

Osteoarthritis (OA) is a progressive degenerative disease that affects the joints. It damages the articular cartilage resulting in limb dysfunction, lameness, and pain. The avascular nature of cartilage contributes to its limited healing potential making it difficult to repair. Mesenchymal stem cells (MSCs) are gaining much attention as a promising therapeutic option in OA due to their ability to secrete paracrine factors that modulate the local immune response, thereby improving chondrocyte survival and proliferation. In addition, specific therapeutic properties of MSCs, such as immunomodulatory, anti-inflammatory, anti-apoptotic, pro-angiogenic, antioxidant, and antimicrobial activity, also contributes to their therapeutic potential. The current research trend indicates a progressive transition from MSC-based therapy to cell-free methods (conditioned media and extracellular vesicle). The rapid advances in cell-based therapies, including the utilization of MSCs and their secretome, will help to provide long-term solutions for cartilage repair and regeneration.

Keywords: Osteoarthritis, Mesenchymal stem cells, Cartilage, Stem cell therapy, Cell-free therapy

Introduction

Osteoarthritis (OA) is a progressive degenerative disease that affects the joints of humans and animals (Belshaw et al., 2020). It causes cartilage damage, meniscal damage, bone remodeling, synovitis, and the formation of osteophytes (Kuppa et al., 2022). It is also associated with the progressive loss of articular cartilage function resulting in limb dysfunction, lameness, and pain (Meeson et al., 2019). Macrophages are directly involved in the inflammatory response associated with OA and are responsible for producing several inflammatory cytokines and chemokines (Kuppa et al., 2022). These pro-inflammatory mediators activate multiple signaling pathways that further recruit more macrophages leading to disease progression (Kuppa et al., 2022). Canine OA is commonly reported in the aged dog population (Meeson et al., 2019; Belshaw et al., 2020). Similarly, knee OA is commonly reported in human medicine. It is mainly managed using strategies such as weight control, therapeutic drugs (non-steroidal anti-inflammatory drugs and opioids), therapeutic exercise, and intraarticular injections (platelet-rich plasma, corticosteroids, and hyaluronic acid (Rodríguez-Merchán, 2022). However, most of these therapeutic strategies relieve joint pain for a shorter duration, making them ineffective.

Being a terminally differentiated tissue, articular cartilage has less self-healing capacity. In addition, the avascular nature of cartilage is also responsible for its limited healing potential (Armiento et al., 2019; Gugjoo et al., 2019). Therefore, once damaged, it is quite difficult to repair articular cartilage. In addition, the repaired tissue will often be mechanically inferior fibrocartilage (Armiento et al., 2019). It has also been found that clinical treatment of cartilage has a limited success rate and often produces mechanically inferior cartilage (Liu et al., 2021). Conventional treatment of OA can be done using joint-preserving strategies in the early phase and joint-replacement therapy towards the end stage (Yu et al., 2022). Although joint-preserving therapy can help alleviate the clinical symptoms associated with OA, it will not prevent the progression of the disease, thereby causing joint pain, dysfunction, and disability in the later stages (Yu et al., 2022). Furthermore, these conventional strategies are not effective enough to block the progression of OA. Therefore, there is a need to understand the pathogenesis of OA further and identify potential targets that can be used to delay the progression of OA (Migliore et al., 2019).

Mesenchymal stem cells (MSCs) are gaining much attention as a promising therapeutic option in the field of regenerative medicine. They are considered a valuable tool for tissue repair due to their high degree of plasticity and their ability to differentiate into multiple lineages (ectoderm, mesoderm, and endoderm) (Prządka et al., 2021). In addition, the paracrine action of MSC-derived secretome is responsible for their anti-inflammatory, antimicrobial, and immunomodulatory activity (Molnar et al., 2022). MSCs are classified according to their relation to the recipient as autogenous, allogeneic, and xenogeneic origin. They are isolated from different tissue sources, such as bone marrow, adipose tissue, dental pulp, birth-related tissues, etc. They are implanted in the target site to stimulate the repair of tissue damage (Berebichez-Fridman et al., 2018). The high cost of operative treatment for OA and the inability of conventional treatment to arrest disease progression have accelerated the research for finding alternative therapeutics (Molnar et al., 2022). This has contributed to the rapid growth in clinical research evaluating the efficacy of MSCs in managing OA. This chapter focuses on the prospects of cell-based and cell-free therapeutic strategies using mesenchymal stem cells for managing osteoarthritis.

Mesenchymal stem cell therapy for osteoarthritis

MSCs are considered a promising cell source for cartilage repair and regeneration due to their ability to differentiate into chondrocytes and ease in collection and expansion from multiple sources with minimal donor site morbidity (Park et al., 2018). Several types of MSCs are currently being used to repair cartilage defects, such as adipose tissue-derived MSCs, bone marrow-derived MSCs, and peripheral blood-derived MSCs (Reissis et al., 2016; Berebichez-Fridman et al., 2018; Liu et al., 2021). The route of administration varies depending on the pathology involved and can be injected via intra-articular injection or implanted into the cartilage defect following a surgical incision (Gugjoo et al. 2016; Gugjoo et al. 2017; Gugjoo et al. 2020; Liu et al., 2021). However, intra-articular injection of MSCs will be associated with a higher risk of the cells migrating to non-target tissues than surgical implantation (Reissis et al., 2016).

Both autologous and allogeneic MSCs isolated from various tissues can ease OA without causing any adverse reactions (Yu et al., 2022). Although several studies have confirmed the therapeutic potential of MSCs in cartilage regeneration and their ability to improve clinical outcomes, several challenges are yet to be corrected before their routine clinical use (Wakitani et al., 2002; Lee et al., 2019). The therapeutic action of MSCs in OA is mediated through three mechanisms: (1) chondrogenic properties of MSCs; (2) paracrine action of growth factors and extracellular vesicles, and (3) anti-inflammatory and immunomodulatory properties of MSCs (Yu et al., 2022).

MSCs exert their regenerative functions by secreting paracrine factors that modulate the local immune response, thereby improving chondrocyte survival and proliferation (Gugjoo and Pal, 2020; Kim et al., 2020; Gugjoo, 2022; Gugjoo et al. 2022;). In addition, MSCs maintain the function and stability of chondrocytes by differentiating into chondrocytes. The MSC-derived exosomes contain many bioactive factors such as mRNA, miRNA, protein, and lipid that helps to treat OA by functioning as intercellular messengers (Yu et al., 2022). Several therapeutic properties of MSCs help to prevent the progression of OA (**Fig. 7.1**). MSCs release different soluble factors that is responsible for specific therapeutic properties such as immunomodulatory, anti-inflammatory, anti-apoptotic, pro-angiogenic, antioxidant, and antimicrobial activity (González-González et al., 2020). The immunomodulatory and anti-inflammatory properties of MSCs and their secretomes mainly contribute to their therapeutic effect in OA (Kuppa et al., 2022). In addition, the anti-apoptotic effects exhibited by MSCs may also play a major role in managing OA, which is mediated through the secretion of hepatocyte growth factor (Wang et al., 2013). Vascular endothelial growth factor (VEGF) is an important angiogenic factor secreted by MSCs that promotes cell survival by inducing the expression Bcl-2. Studies have found that Bcl-2 mediates the regulation of chondrocyte apoptosis in OA (Murata et al., 2008). MSCs also secrete granulocyte-macrophage colony-stimulating factor that inhibits cellular apoptosis and restores tissue homeostasis (Fan et al., 2020).

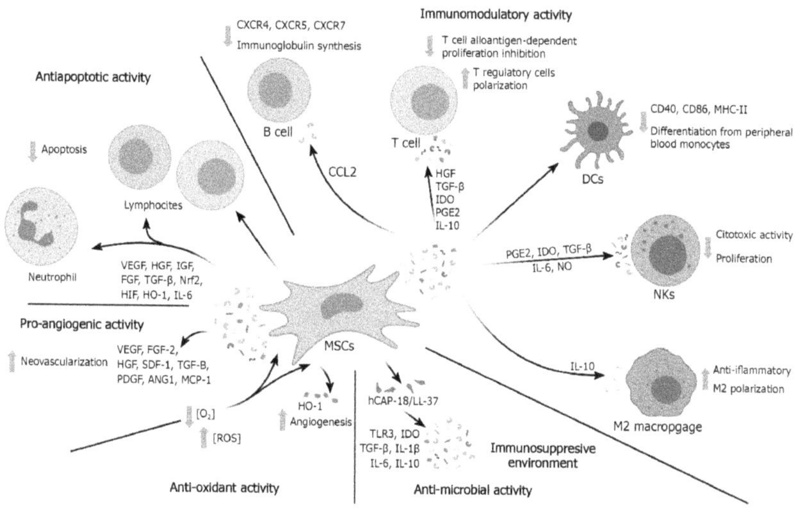

Fig. 7.1: Overview of the different soluble factors secreted by mesenchymal stem cells and their contribution to different therapeutic properties. Reproduced from González-González et al. (2020) under Creative Commons Attribution Non-Commercial (CC BY-NC 4.0) license.

Compared to other categories of stem cells, MSCs have several advantages, especially over embryonic stem cells in terms of an ethical standpoint. Similarly, the widespread use of induced pluripotent stem cells is limited due to their teratogenic potential (Gorecka et al., 2019). Furthermore, MSCs are isolated from different tissue sources such as bone marrow, adipose tissue, dental pulp, and birth-related tissues (Berebichez-Fridman et al., 2018). Among the different sources of MSCs, adipose-derived MSCs have recently received much attention for managing musculoskeletal pathologies, including osteoarthritis (Sharun et al., 2022a).

Human clinical trials

Bone marrow concentrate contains a large amount of MSCs (Kim et al., 2020). A recent clinical trial evaluated the safety and efficacy of autologous bone marrow aspirate concentrate in treating knee osteoarthritis (Mariani et al., 2022). The findings indicate that a single intra-articular injection of bone marrow aspirate concentrate is safe and beneficial for managing knee osteoarthritis based on the patient-reported outcome measures (Mariani et al., 2022). Furthermore, the safety and efficacy of combined MSC and platelet-rich plasma in the treatment of knee OA were evaluated using meta-analysis (Zhao et al., 2022). The combined use of MSCs and platelet-rich plasma was associated with improved pain and joint function in patients with knee OA resulting in good clinical outcomes. However, no significant difference was observed in the incidence of adverse reactions when using MSCs as monotherapy (Zhao et al., 2022).

Similarly, intra-articular injection of MSCs can also be combined with scaffolds for the management of knee OA (Wu et al., 2022). In addition, MSCs have certain properties that contribute to the therapeutic potential in OA, such as immunomodulatory activity, inhibit inflammatory factor release, promote tissue repair, and increase in the healing potential of injured cells (Fu et al., 2019; Wu et al., 2022). In addition, they also possess the ability for multidirectional differentiation, secreting a broad spectrum of cytokines (paracrine activity) that contributes to anti-fibrosis, anti-inflammatory, anti-apoptosis, pro-angiogenesis, and pro-mitosis properties (Fu et al., 2019).

Animal clinical trials

Studies evaluating the extracellular vesicle proteome in osteoarthritic synovial fluid following MSC treatment are scarce. However, the findings from a recent study in horses with experimentally induced OA suggest that extracellular vesicles mediate its therapeutic action through altered joint homeostasis (Clarke et al., 2022). Similarly, *in vivo* experiments using a rat OA model found that microRNA-376c-3p present in human adipose MSC-derived exosomes mitigated chondrocyte degradation and synovial fibrosis associated with OA suggesting prospects in the clinical application (Li et al., 2022). In addition, intra-articular injection of peripheral blood-derived MSCs inhibited cartilage degradation and inflammation in trauma-induced OA mice models preventing its progression (Lin et al., 2022). In another study, the mechanism of human adipose-derived MSCs in OA management was studied using OA hulth model in Sprague Dawley rats (Xu et al., 2022). The findings indicate that MSCs delay OA progression in rats and improve the associated pathological changes in joints. In addition, human adipose-derived MSCs inhibited the expression of Caspase1, NLR family pyrin domain containing 3 (NLRP3), tumor necrosis factor receptor 1 (TNFR1), and Gasdermin D (GSDMD).

Cell-free strategies for osteoarthritis

It was initially thought that the therapeutic effects of MSCs were because of their ability to undergo differentiation into multiple cell types at the site of injury, thereby replacing damaged or diseased tissues (Salem and Thiemermann, 2010). However, it was later found that the paracrine secretions of MSCs were responsible for their therapeutic effects (González-González et al., 2020; Maacha et al., 2020). These paracrine secretions are collectively called as the secretome and consist of soluble proteins, extracellular vesicles, growth factors, free nucleic acids, and lipids (Maacha et al., 2020).

Cell-free strategies based on MSCs (conditioned media and extracellular vesicles) are gaining momentum and can be considered the future of MSC-based therapy (Sharun et al., 2022b). It has several advantages over cell-based therapy, such as low immunogenicity and off-shelf availability. Furthermore, cell-free therapy lacks disadvantages such as low cell survival and unpredictable behavior, making them a safe alternative to cell-based therapeutics (Sharun et al., 2022c). The composition of the MSC secretome and the extracellular vesicle cargo can be modified according to our need to suit specific therapeutic goals (González-González et al., 2020).

Conclusion and prospects

Our understanding of MSCs and their therapeutic potential have improved significantly over the past decade. MSCs have already established their therapeutic potential in articular cartilage regeneration and repair. The current research trend indicates a progressive transition from MSC-based therapy to cell-free methods (conditioned media and extracellular vesicle). However, due to the limited data, it is too early to comment on the efficacy of MSC-based cell-free therapy for managing osteoarthritis. The rapid advances in cell-based therapies, including the utilization of MSCs and their secretome, will help to provide long-term solutions for cartilage repair and regeneration. However, the financial costs associated with MSC therapy must be reduced with future research to make it easily available to every human and veterinary patient.

References

1. Armiento AR, et al. (2019). Ar ticular fibrocartilage - Why does hyaline cartilage fail to repair? Adv Drug Deliv Rev 146: 289-305.
2. Belshaw Z, et al. (2020). Could it be osteoarthritis? How dog owners and veterinary surgeons describe identifying canine osteoarthritis in a general practice setting. Prev Vet Med 185: 105198.
3. Berebichez-Fridman R, & Montero-Olvera PR. (2018). Sources and Clinical Applications of Mesenchymal Stem Cells: State-of-the-art

review. Sultan Qaboos Univ Med J 18(3):e264-e277.

4. Clarke EJ, et al. (2022). Temporal extracellular vesicle protein changes following intraarticular treatment with integrin α10β1-selected mesenchymal stem cells in equine osteoarthritis. Front Vet Sci 9: 1057667.
5. Fan XL, et al. (2020). Mechanisms underlying the protective effects of mesenchymal stem cell-based therapy. Cell Mol Life Sci 77(14): 2771-2794.
6. Fu X, et al. (2019). Mesenchymal Stem Cell Migration and Tissue Repair. Cells 8(8): 784.
7. González-González A, et al. (2020). Mesenchymal stem cells secretome: The cornerstone of cell-free regenerative medicine. World J Stem Cells 12(12): 1529-1552.
8. Gorecka J, Kostiuk V, et al. (2019). The potential and limitations of induced pluripotent stem cells to achieve wound healing. Stem Cell Res Ther 10(1): 87.
9. Gugjoo MB, et al. (2017). Mesenchymal stem cells with IGF-1 and TGF-β1 in laminin gel for osteochondral defects in rabbits. Biomed Pharmacother 93: 1165-1174.
10. Gugjoo MB, et al. (2016). Cartilage tissue engineering: Role of Mesenchymal stem cells along with growthfactors and scaffolds. Indian J Med Res. 144: 339-347.
11. Gugjoo MB, et al. (2019). Animal mesenchymal stem cell research in cartilage regenerative medicine - a review. Vet Quarterly 39(1):95-120.
12. Gugjoo et al. (2020). Allogeneic Mesenchymal Stem Cells and Growth Factors In Gel Scaffold Repair Osteochondral Defect in Rabbit. Reg Med. 15(2): 1261-1275.
13. Gugjoo et al. (2022). Cryopreserved Allogeneic Bone marrow Mesenchymal Stem Cells show Better Osteochondral Defect Repair Potential than Adipose Tissue Mesenchymal stem cells. Current Res Transl Med. 2022: 103364.
14. Kim GB, et al. (2020). Bone Marrow Aspirate Concentrate: Its Uses in Osteoarthritis. Int J Mol Sci 21(9):3224.
15. Kim YG, et al. (2020). Mesenchymal Stem Cell-Derived Exosomes for Effective Cartilage Tissue Repair and Treatment of Osteoarthritis. Biotechnol J 15(12): e2000082.
16. Kuppa SS, et al. (2022). Role of Mesenchymal Stem Cells and Their Paracrine Mediators in Macrophage Polarization: An Approach to

Reduce Inflammation in Osteoarthritis. Int J Mol Sci 23(21): 13016.

17. Lee WS, et al. (2019). Intra-Articular Injection of Autologous Adipose Tissue-Derived Mesenchymal Stem Cells for the Treatment of Knee Osteoarthritis: A Phase IIb, Randomized, Placebo-Controlled Clinical Trial. Stem Cells Transl Med 8(6): 504-511.
18. Li F, et al. (2022). Adipose mesenchymal stem cells-derived exosomes alleviate osteoarthritis by transporting microRNA -376c-3p and targeting the WNT-beta-catenin signaling axis. Apoptosis 2022.
19. Lin W, et al. (2022). Alleviation of osteoarthritis by intra-articular transplantation of circulating mesenchymal stem cells. Biochem Biophys Res Commun. 636(Pt 1): 25-32.
20. Liu Y, et al. (2021). Strategies for Articular Cartilage Repair and Regeneration. Front Bioeng Biotechnol 9: 770655.
21. Maacha S, et al. (2020). Paracrine Mechanisms of Mesenchymal Stromal Cells in Angiogenesis. Stem Cells Int 2020: 4356359.
22. Mariani C, et al. (2022). Use of bone marrow derived mesenchymal stem cells for the treatment of osteoarthritis: A retrospective long-term follow-up study. J Clin Orthop Trauma 36: 102084.
23. Meeson RL, et al. (2019). Spontaneous dog osteoarthritis - a One Medicine vision. Nat Rev Rheumatol 15(5): 273-287.
24. Migliore A, et al. (2019). Treat-to-target strategy for knee osteoarthritis. International technical expert panel consensus and good clinical practice statements. Ther Adv Musculoskelet Dis 11: 1759720X19893800.
25. Molnar V, et al. (2022). Mesenchymal Stem Cell Mechanisms of Action and Clinical Effects in Osteoarthritis: A Narrative Review. Genes (Basel). 13(6):949.
26. Murata M, et al. (2008). The potential role of vascular endothelial growth factor (VEGF) in cartilage: how the angiogenic factor could be involved in the pathogenesis of osteoarthritis? Osteoarthritis Cartilage 16(3): 279-86.
27. Park YB, et al. (2018). Stem Cell Therapy for Articular Cartilage Repair: Review of the Entity of Cell Populations Used and the Result of the Clinical Application of Each Entity. Am J Sports Med 46(10): 2540-2552.
28. Prządka P, et al. (2021). The Role of Mesenchymal Stem Cells (MSCs) in Veterinary Medicine and Their Use in Musculoskeletal Disorders. Biomol 11(8):1141.
29. Reissis D, et al. (2016). Current clinical evidence for the use of mesenchymal stem cells in articular cartilage repair. Expert Opin Biol

Ther 16(4): 535-57.

30. Rodríguez-Merchán EC. (2022). Intraarticular Injections of Mesenchymal Stem Cells in Knee Osteoarthritis: A Review of Their Current Molecular Mechanisms of Action and Their Efficacy. Int J Mol Sci 2(23): 14953.
31. Salem HK & Thiemermann C. (2010). Mesenchymal stromal cells: current understanding and clinical status. Stem Cells. 28(3): 585-96.
32. Sharun K, et al. (2022c). Cell-free Therapy for Inflammatory Diseases: Opportunities and Challenges. Recent Adv Inflamm Allergy Drug Discov 15(1): 5-8.
33. Sharun K, et al. (2022a). Mapping global trends in adipose-derived mesenchymal stem cell research: A bibliometric analysis using scopus database. Ann Med Surg (Lond) 77: 103542.
34. Sharun K, et al (2022b). Cell-free therapy for canine osteoarthritis: current evidence and prospects. Vet Quarterly 42(1): 224-230.
35. Wakitani S, et al. (2002. Human autologous culture expanded bone marrow mesenchymal cell transplantation for repair of cartilage defects in osteoarthritic knees. Osteoarthritis Cartilage 10(3): 199-206.
36. Wang H, et al. (2013). Hepatocyte growth factor gene-modified mesenchymal stem cells reduce radiation-induced lung injury. Hum Gene Ther 24(3): 343-53.
37. Wu Q, et al. (2022). Clinical efficacy and safety of the combination of mesenchymal stem cells and scaffolds in the treatment of knee osteoarthritis: Protocol for systematic review and meta-analysis. Medicine (Baltimore) 101(43): e31638.
38. Xu L, et al. (2022). Attenuation of experimental osteoarthritis with human adipose-derived mesenchymal stem cell therapy: inhibition of the pyroptosis in chondrocytes. Inflamm Res. 2022 Nov 4.
39. Yu H, et al. (2022). Research progress in the use of mesenchymal stem cells and their derived exosomes in the treatment of osteoarthritis. Ageing Res Rev 80: 101684.
40. Zhao J, et al. (2022). Combination of mesenchymal stem cells (MSCs) and platelet-rich plasma (PRP) in the treatment of knee osteoarthritis: a meta-analysis of randomised controlled trials. BMJ Open 12(11): e061008.

CHAPTER EIGHT

Mesenchymal Stem Cells for Metabolic Syndrome

Uzair Bashir and Saboora Saleem

Department of Clinical Biochemistry, University of Kashmir, Hazratbal, Srinagar, J&K, India

Abstract

The complex clinical condition known as metabolic syndrome, which has its roots in obesity and is associated with a significant risk of cardiovascular disease and mortality, has spread like an epidemic throughout the world. The main components of metabolic syndrome include dyslipidemia, hypertension, diabetes, or glucose dysmetabolism. These components are interconnected and have common pathophysiological pathways. Individuals who have severe obesity are more likely to develop metabolic syndrome, and current research indicates that mesenchymal stem cells (MSCs) play a key role in adipocyte formation by increasing the number of adipocytes. In light of this, a growing number of researches have looked into the possible contributions that MSCs could make to the treatment of obesity and metabolic syndrome. The efficacy and safety of MSCs in the therapeutic context still need to be optimized, despite the expanding body of experimental and clinical data. Thus, it is hoped that ongoing and future research may shed light on the functions of MSCs in metabolic syndrome and result in MSC-based treatment options for those who are affected. Current knowledge of the connection between MSCs and the metabolic syndrome is discussed, along with any potential implications for patient therapy.

Keywords: Metabolic syndrome, mesenchymal stem cells, therapeutic

Introduction

The metabolic syndrome is a complicated triad of obesity-related problems that has recently gained attention as a major global health issue. The primary components of metabolic syndrome are dyslipidaemia, hypertension, and diabetes or glucose dysmetabolism. These components are interconnected and have common pathophysiological pathways. Patients with severe obesity are more likely to develop metabolic syndrome, which increases their risk of cardiovascular disease and mortality (NCEP, 2001; Haffner & Taegtmeyer, 2003; Alberti et al. 2009).

According to recent research, mesenchymal stem cells (MSCs) constitute a significant source of adipocyte development, leading to an increase in the number of adipocytes. Numerous adult tissues, including bone marrow, adipose tissue, the umbilical cord, the endometrium, skeletal muscle, pancreas, and liver cells, can produce MSCs. Therefore, substantial research has been done on the biology of MSCs, their ability to treat a variety of disorders, and their potential involvement in regulating the many aspects of metabolic syndrome. MSC-based clinical trials have also been completed or are still being conducted, despite the specific nature and roles of MSCs still being unknown. However, the safety and efficacy of MSCs, which have yet to be refined, are essential for therapeutic uses in the clinical context. This review examines the present state of knowledge about the connection between MSCs and metabolic syndrome, as well as any potential ramifications for employing MSCs to treat people who have the condition.

The Cellular Perspective

Cellular therapy could offer a revolutionary viewpoint for comprehending and treating difficult clinical conditions like metabolic syndrome, among many others. Few people are aware of the connection between lipodystrophies and metabolic syndrome. Adipose tissue loss is a characteristic of both congenital lipodystrophies (such as Emery Dreyfuss muscular dystrophy, Dunnigan-type familial partial lipodystrophy, and Berardinelli Seip syndrome) and acquired lipodystrophies (such as HIV-associated lipodystrophy and cachexia associated with neoplasia's). In addition, these disorders are characterized by insulin resistance, fatty liver disease, and hyperlipidemia. In lipodystrophies, apoptosis leads in a continuous and severe loss of adipocytes, impairing the metabolism of free fatty acids and causing major organic effects such lipotoxicity, which are directly related to the start of metabolic syndrome. On the other hand, obesity or increased adiposity is the cause of the increased release of fat metabolites. These include glycerol, interleukin-6 (IL-6), free fatty acids

(FFA), tumor necrosis factor-alpha (TNF-), plasminogen activator inhibitor-1 (PAI-1), and active C-reactive protein (CRP). It was shown that the released FFAs disrupted the phosphoinositide 3-kinase (PI3K)-Akt pathway, which controls a number of intracellular regulatory processes like cell proliferation and death. It was found that inflammation caused by obesity plays a crucial role in the development of insulin resistance in type 2 diabetes (T2DM). Examples of highly active metabolic tissues that display insulin resistance in T2DM include the liver, fat, and muscles. The NOD-like receptor protein 3 (NLRP3) is a key player in both the inflammatory response and activities mediated by insulin. The inflammasome carries NLRP3 as well as caspase-1 and apoptosis-associated speck-like protein (ASC). NLRP3 functionally interacts with ASC to activate caspase-1. Caspase-1 promotes cellular maturation and the production of cytokines that cause inflammation (IL-1 and IL-18). The absence of insulin-mediated regulation increases unregulated lipogenesis and the production of reactive oxygen species in addition to localized macrophage activity (ROS).

Mesenchymal stem cells

The study of stem cells has given rise to the fascinating new branch of research known as regenerative medicine. Regenerative medicine is a subfield of translational research that aims to repair damaged tissues and restore their ability to function normally (Lee et al., 2004; Bernardo et al., 2012). The cell type that has been investigated in clinical trials the most frequently so far is mesenchymal stem/stromal cells (MSCs). MSCs have the potential to be employed in therapy since they are simple to isolate, can differentiate into many cell types, don't elicit an immune response, and—most significantly—release biological substances that aid in the healing of damaged tissues (Ding et al., 2015). Multipotent stem cells (MSCs) originate in the mesoderm. They typically exhibit certain surface antigen markers (CD73, CD90, and CD105), cling to plastic and keep reproducing themselves, and at the absolute least have the capacity to transform into osteocytes, adipocytes, or chondrocytes (Pittenger et al., 1999; Dominica et al., 2006). Since MSCs are present throughout the body, they can be extracted from a variety of tissues, including bone marrow, heart, skin, bodily fluids, and perinatal tissues. When their milieu (pH, oxygen, and stress) changes, MSCs respond by releasing immune-modulating and trophic substances that promote the repair of injured cells and tissues. The MSCs created from the umbilical cords Wharton's Jelly demonstrated that MSCs can also be produced to secrete immunosuppressive and cytoprotective substances (WJ-MSC). These MSC have recently gained favor as a viable option for stem cell-based treatment to treat a variety of disorders. Contrary to what the majority of sites claim, WJ-MSCs are simple to obtain from waste tissues and call for little to no invasive procedures. Therefore, neither the parent's nor the child's safety is in jeopardy or in danger. WJ-MSCs are derived from nascent tissues rather than mature or adult tissue sources because they have a stronger capacity for cell proliferation, contain immunosuppressive factors, and are therapeutically active with little genetic alterations brought on by ageing and disease. MSCs and the factors they produce have demonstrated excellent therapeutic effects in the treatment of a number of illnesses, and they are currently being explored for the treatment of MetS and illnesses connected to it.

MSCs in MetS

In *in-vivo* models, investigation has been done and role of MSCs in the treatment of T1DM, T2DM, PAH, diabetic cardiomyopathy (DC), and diabetic nephropathy (DN) (El-Badri & Ghoneim, 2013; Gugjoo, 2022). Treatment options for T1DM brought on by the demise of insulin-producing cells were examined in 12 studies (Davani et al. 2007). The other studies examined T2DM brought on by insulin resistance in two, PAH brought on by endothelial dysfunction in two, DC, a region without coronary artery disease, and DN brought on by high glucose levels that harm the kidneys in one. The research either utilised animals fed a high-fat diet (HFD), diabetic animals given streptozotocin (STZ), or high blood pressure animals given monocrotaline (MCT). Rats or mice were utilised as test subjects in the research. The C54/BL6 mouse was utilised in four research, the BALB/c mouse in three, the NOD/SCID mouse in two, and the naked mouse in one. In five of the rat investigations, Sprague-Dawley rats were utilised, while Wistar, Kunming, and albino rats were employed in each of the other three studies. Female mice were only employed in one of the investigations. In most research, male animals were employed. Additionally, the majority of the research (n=13) used STZ intraperitoneal injections to make animal models of diabetes. The other diabetic models were brought on by either a high-fat diet (HFD), an intracardial injection of STZ, or both an HFD and an intracardial injection of STZ. MCT injections were used in two trials to simulate PAH in animals. MSC transplantation improved survival rates, insulin levels, and glucose tolerance in diabetic rats by correcting hyperglycemia, maintaining body weight, and enhancing glucose tolerance. MSC transplantation increased the size and pressure of the ventricles in the hypertension animals. The places where the heart, lungs, thymus, liver, spleen, and kidneys function are where the MSCs that were administered were discovered. The MSCs typically travelled to the harmed tissue and regions and performed well there. Abdominal obesity is a common cause of MetS and is related to it (Shen et al., 2015). People can become obese for a variety of reasons, including what they eat, how much exercise they get, whether or not they smoke, and their family history. Weight gain, high blood sugar, high insulin levels, pancreatic cell loss, insulin resistance, dyslipidemia, inflammation, and fibrosis are pathological alterations that occur in people with MetS (Rosen & MacDougald, 2006). Because SCs have the ability to transform into many cell types and have self-healing capabilities, they are a very promising novel treatment for T1D. Based on their origins, SCs can be divided into four major groupings (**Fig. 8.1**).

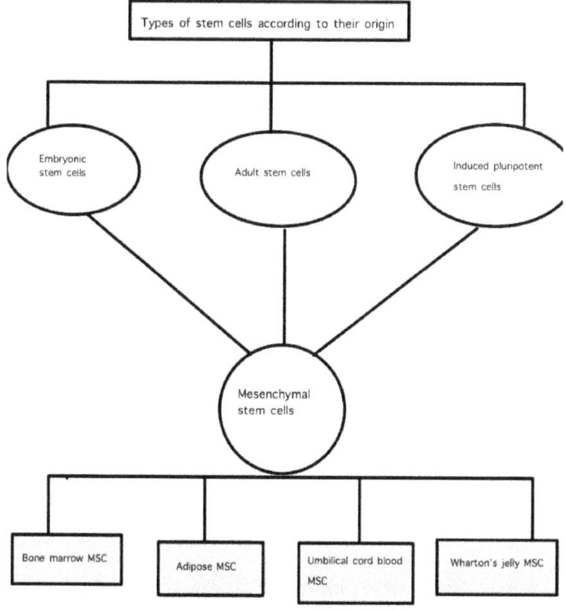

Fig.1: Classification of stem cells based on their origin

The restoration of -cell function and the reversal of inflammatory damage are the two main functions of MSCs. MSCs concentrate on inflammatory and damaged sites before secreting bioactive chemicals to establish an environment that would promote -cell regeneration and inhibit T cell-mediated immune responses. However, following transplantation, MSCs do not differentiate into -cells since there is no evidence of the right ventricular form and function, blood pressure, or pulmonary vasculature. Some studies have shown that MSCs enhance islet regeneration. Cardiovascular disease and acute lung injury may be affected by MSCs. Early MSCs therapy improves lung health and may have generated paracrine chemicals that influenced where collagen was located in the cardiopulmonary system. MSCs have an anti-GVHD effect by suppressing the immune system and controlling T cells. This finding reveals that MSCs can help wounded vascular and alveolar cells repair by acting as immunoregulators. MSCs have a number of benefits over chemical medications, including a decrease in pulmonary arteriole thickening and the expression of numerous genes. Chemical medications are unable to arrest the progression of the disease or reduce mortality. MSCs are thought to be helpful in addition by increasing anti-inflammatory cytokines, eliciting a positive sympathetic response, and altering the cardiopulmonary system. Several mechanisms have been discovered to play a role in the management of T1D by MSCs (**Fig. 8.2**).

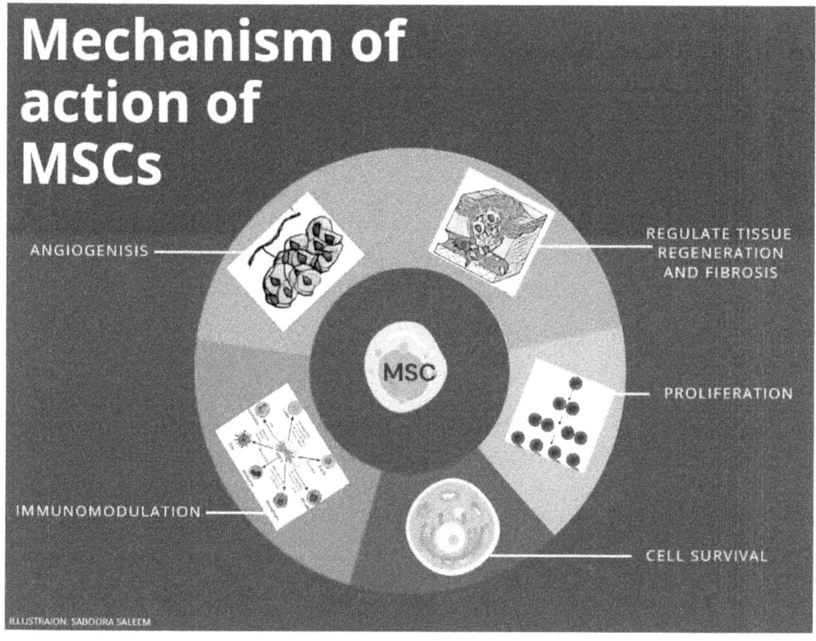

Fig. 2: Mechanisms of action of MSCs

Future Perspectives

For potential clinical application, a deeper comprehension of how MSC adipogenesis links to each disorder that makes up metabolic syndrome is unquestionably of paramount importance. The process of adipogenesis itself is extremely intricate. Additionally, the connection between adipogenesis and obesity is linked to the regulation of inflammatory cytokines and cellular processes such mitochondrial biogenesis in addition to cellular differentiation. Additionally, the complicated pathophysiology of metabolic syndrome and the precise processes connecting each condition are yet unknown, which restricts the available therapeutic choices. As a result, the prospective uses of MSCs in the treatment of metabolic syndrome offer great promise for patients (**Fig. 8.3**).

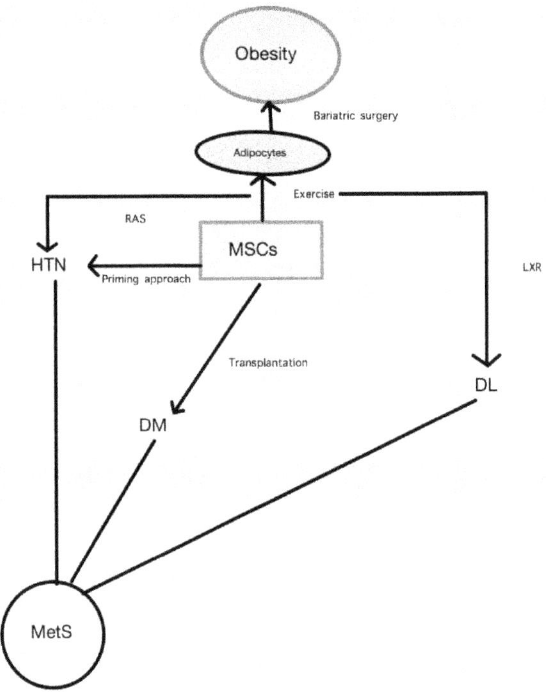

Fig. 3: Scheme of the clinical impact of MSC adipogenesis on metabolic syndrome. Pathophysiology of metabolic syndrome is quite complex and the precise mechanisms linking each condition remain unclear. Among the potential clinical applications of MSCs, studies assessing MSCs as a source of transplantation material in the treatment of diabetes have shown encouraging results. MSC-based therapeutic options for diabetes could be used in the clinical setting in the future. Although further studies are needed to elucidate the roles of MSCs and MSC adipogenesis in metabolic syndrome, MSC therapy is expected to become a new level of therapeutic option for this syndrome. DL, dyslipidemia; DM, diabetes mellitus; HTN, hypertension; LXRs, liver X receptors; MetS, metabolic syndrome; MSCs, mesenchymal stem cells; and RAS, renin-angiotensin system.

In order to address the safety and efficacy concerns relating to the clinical applications of MSCs, more clinical trials including bigger patient populations and longer monitoring times are now required. MSC treatment is anticipated to advance as a therapeutic option for metabolic syndrome in the future.

Conclusion

The complex clinical disorder known as metabolic syndrome, which is based on obesity, has spread like an epidemic throughout the world. Current therapy options for people with metabolic syndrome are scarce, and the underlying pathophysiology of this illness is still poorly understood. Studies are being conducted to determine the potential functions of MSCs in the therapy of obesity and metabolic syndrome as well as their safety and efficacy in the therapeutic context. MSCs are thought to be a key source of adipocyte production. A successful MSC therapy for individuals with the metabolic syndrome may be developed with further understanding of the biology of MSCs and their functions in this illness.

References

1. "Executive summary of the third report of the National Cholesterol Education Program (NCEP) expert panel on detection, evaluation, and treatment of high blood cholesterol in adults (adult treatment panel III)," J Am Med Assoc 285(19): 2486–2497. 2001.
2. Alberti KG, et al. (2009). "Harmonizing the metabolic syndrome: a joint interim statement of the international diabetes federation task force on epidemiology and prevention; National heart, lung, and blood institute; American heart association; World heart federation; International atherosclerosis society; And international association for the study of obesity. Circulation 120(16): 1640–1645.
3. Bernardo ME, et al. (2012). "Mesenchymal stromal cell therapy: a revolution in Regenerative Medicine," Bone Marrow Transplant 47(2): 164–171.
4. Davani B, et al. (2007). "Human islet-derived precursor cells are mesenchymal stromal cells that differentiate and mature to hormone-expressing cells in vivo," StemCells 25(12): 3215–3222.
5. Ding D-C, et al. (2015). "Human umbilical cord mesenchymal stem cells: a new era for stem cell therapy," Cell Transplant 24(3): 339–347.
6. El-Badri N. & Ghoneim MA. (2013). "Mesenchymal stem cell therapy in diabetes mellitus: progress and challenges," J Nucleic Acids 2013:

194858.

7. Gugjoo Mb. (2022). Mesenchymal Stem Cells Therapeutic Applications in Endocrine Disorders. In: Therapeutic Applications of Mesenchymal Stem Cells in Veterinary Medicine. Springer Nature. pp. 375-390.
8. Haffner S, & Taegtmeyer H. (2003). "Epidemic obesity and the metabolic syndrome," Circulation 108(13): 1541–1545.
9. Lee RH, et al. (2004). "Characterization and expression analysis of mesenchymal stem cells from human bone marrow and adipose tissue," Cell Physiol Biochem 14(4–6): 311–324.
10. Pittenger MF, et al. (1999). "Multilineage potential of adult human mesenchymal stem cells," Science 284(5411): 143–147.
11. Rosen ED, & MacDougald OA. (2006). "Adipocyte differentiation from the inside out," Nature Reviews: Mol Cell Biol 7(12): 885–896.
12. Shen H, et al. (2015). "High density lipoprotein promotes proliferation of adipose-derived stem cells via S1P1 receptor and Akt, ERK1/2 signal pathways," Stem Cell Res Therapy 61): 95.

CHAPTER NINE

Mesenchymal Stem Cells for Intervertebral Disc Degeneration

Ibtisam Mumtaz

Laboratory of Regenerative Medicine and Nano-Therapeutics, University of Kashmir, Hazratbal, Srinagar, J&K, India

Abstract

Although the severity of intervertebral disc degeneration (IVDD) rises with age, it can also affect people who are younger. Its recurrence has a negative impact on the patient's health and financial situation. Currently, a variety of conventional techniques are utilized to reduce pain and alleviate symptoms, but each of these techniques has its own drawbacks. Due to this, a more sophisticated kind of treatment is required, one that aims to regenerate the deteriorated intervertebral disc (IVD) rather than replace the already present IVD. Globally, significant efforts are made to create cell-based treatment strategies and the utilization of mesenchymal stem cells.

Keywords: Intervertebral disc degeneration, Inter-vertebral disc, Cell-based treatment, Mesenchymal Stem Cells.

Introduction

Low back pain (LBP) always remains a difficult condition to treat and to cure. It is the second most typical symptom in the US. 85% of people in the US experience chronic LBP at some point in their lifetime. Although LBP usually occurs in females between the ages of 35 and 80 years, but there is no age group spared from this problem and also a huge number of children worldwide suffer from it (Hoy et al., 2012). It is also a major cause of economic burden in the US, leading to expenses between $100 and

$200 billion per year (Katz, 2006). The main causes of LBP are vertebral fractures, spinal tumours, infections and intervertebral disc degeneration (IDD). Among these IDD is the major cause of LBP (Cheung et al., 2009; Golob et al., 2014; Hartvigsen et al. 2018). IDD also accounts for Degenerative disc diseases (DDDs) which comprise painful spinal diseases including lumbar disc herniation and discogenic low back pain (Battié et al., 1976).

The shielded structure of the intervertebral Disc and how it degenerates

The intervertebral disc is a solid structure that is placed between two adjacent vertebrae. It confers flexibility to the spinal cord and also helps in movement. An IVD is a cylindrical structure, which comprises three distinct regions, nucleus pulposus (NP) which is the well-hydrated central region, a flexible collageneous lamella surrounding the NP called the annulus fibrosis (AF) and the cartilaginous end plates (CEPs). The NP is rich in proteoglycans and Collagen type 2 (Vickers et al., 2018). IVD degenerates as a result of matrix loss because of an alteration in the cellular metabolism and due to an imbalance between the synthesis of a matrix and its breakdown. The advancement of IVD degeneration results in the replacement of Collagen type 2 with Collagen type 1 (Roughley, 2004). The proteoglycan levels also decrease which reduces the water binding capacity that in turn makes the NP more condensed and Fibrous. The degradation of the matrix is also accelerated by the upregulation of matrix metalloproteases (MMPs) which are matrix-degrading enzymes. Increased NP cell apoptosis and senescence are two other cellular alterations that occur in conjunction with the deterioration of the matrix. These events altogether disintegrate the structure of the NP and also reduce the height of the disc which ultimately decreases the ability of the disc to withstand any load. Any load on the degenerated disc later leads to fissures in the disc through the AF region. These fissures cause disc herniation which is accompanied by the ingrowth of blood vessels and nervous supply in the disc (**Fig. 9.1**). Herniation of the disc thus causes the sensation of chronic LBP (Vickers et al., 2018).

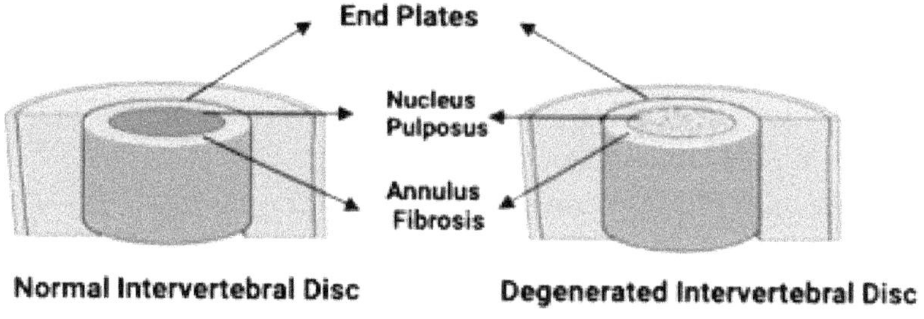

Fig. 9.1: Image showing a normal intervertebral disc and a degenerated disc

Conservative treatment methods for IDD

Currently, the majority of patients are treated with conservative techniques of pain management as well as medications such as NSAIDs, steroid analgesics, different blocking agents, and local anaesthetics (Wentao et al., 2022). When these medications don't work as well as they should, more invasive interventions like surgeries are frequently needed to relieve the symptoms. Currently, spinal fusion is frequently performed after discectomy, the "gold standard" procedure for treating IDD (De Kunder et al., 2018). This technique involves surgically removing the deteriorated IVD and then filling the empty space between the two adjacent vertebral bodies with bone grafts or other materials that can be enhanced with osteogenic growth factors like BMP2 (Bone Morphogenetic Factor 2) (De Kunder et al., 2018). Pedicle screws are then inserted between the two vertebral bodies in order to increase their mechanical stability and improve mobility between the two vertebral bodies (May et al., 2019). Although discectomy can treat pain issues, it also has disadvantages, including the inability to change IVD's pathological state, its high invasiveness, and the possibility of a number of intraoperative and postoperative complications and infections (Pan et al., 2020, Kim et al., 2020).

The Role of Stem cell-based therapies in IVDD

Stem cells are specialised cells with the capacity to regenerate and develop into numerous cell types. They have relatively low immunogenicity and are widely available. Around the world, stem cells have been employed in the treatment of numerous ailments. These cells have been employed to stop the progression of IVDD or achieve IVD repair in the therapy of IVDD. Mesenchymal stem cells (MSCs), embryonic stem cells (ESCs), induced pluripotent stem cells, and intervertebral disc-derived stem cells (IVDSCs) are just a few of the stem cell types that have been used to treat IVDD etc (Wentao et al., 2022).

Mesenchymal Cells in the therapeutics of IVDD

A deteriorated IVD can be treated with stem cells in various different ways. Stem cells have the capacity to develop into NP- or IVD-like cells and produce new ECM (Sakai et al., 2005; Richardson et al., 2006; Le Maitre et al., 2009). In some circumstances, stem cells can help to improve resistance in cells and increase their viability by secreting specific growth factors, chemokines, and anti-inflammatory compounds (Vadalà et al., 2008; Gugjoo et al. 2019; Gugjoo, 2022). These cells can also modulate the immune system by releasing anti-inflammatory cytokines, growth factors, anti-metabolic mediators etc. This is quite helpful in counteracting the inflammatory response shown upon ECM degradation during IDD (Borem et al., 2019).

The term "mesenchymal stromal cells" also refers to mesenchymal stem cells. The osteoblasts, chondrocytes, and adipocytes that can develop from these multipotent stem cells are only a few examples (Horst et al., 2020). MSCs can be isolated from almost all parts of the body e.g Bone marrow, umbilical cord, adipose tissue, Cord blood, etc. Mesenchymal stem cells produced from bone marrow can regenerate IVD cells by encouraging their own self-replication and boosting the production of Collagen type 1, proteoglycans, and other ECM substances (Zhan et al., 2018). According to research, transforming growth factor (TGF-1) and the bone morphogenetic proteins BMP-7, BMP-3, and TGF-1 can cause BM-MSCs to differentiate into NP-like cells (Han et al., 2015; Zhou et al., 2015; Xu et al., 2016). When AD-MSCs are cultured with TGF- 3, more IVD cells and ECM components are found in the cells (Jin et al., 2013). Similar to BM-MSCs, AD-MSCs can develop into NP cells, produce a variety of growth factors, and participate in IVD regeneration and repair.

Wharton's jelly is where most umbilical cord mesenchymal stem cells (UC-MSCs) are found. These stem cells have a low immunogenicity, a high rate of differentiation, and rapid multiplication. According to studies, UC-MSCs boost the expression of proteoglycans and collagen type 2 in NP cells while also encouraging the creation of the extracellular matrix (Qi et al.,

2019). UC-MSCs and degenerative NP cells were put into a scaffold in an experiment, and a rabbit IDD model was used to study the results. It was discovered that this combination boosted IVD healing by encouraging UC-MSCs development in NP-like cells and preventing cell leakage both during and after implantation (Beeravolu et al., 2018). Thus, MSCs have a quite promising role in the regeneration or repair of degenerated IVD. However, the significant outcome can confirmed in clinical trials that remains to be undertaken.

Conclusion

To treat discogenic Lower Back Pain, spinal fusion has historically been regarded as the "gold standard." However, this procedure is only able to replace the degraded IVD; it cannot be repaired. In addition, these surgeries are extremely invasive and are linked to both intraoperative and postoperative infections. A lot of work is being put into creating biological treatments that can restore the IVD that has degraded. Scientists from all over the world are interested in using stem cell-based therapies, particularly MSC-based therapies because of how simple it is to extract them and because of how multipotent they are, to cure IVDs that have deteriorated. In numerous investigations to date, growth factors have been introduced externally to these cells to induce an IVD-like phenotype, enhancing the MSCs compatibility.

References:

1. Battié MC, et al. (1976). Degenerative disc disease: What is in a name? Spine 44(21): 1523-1529.
2. Beeravolu N, et al. (2018). Human umbilical cord derivatives regenerate intervertebral disc. J Tissue Eng Regen Med 12(1): e579-e591.
3. Borem R, et al. (2019). Differential effector response of amnion- and adipose-derived mesenchymal stem cells to inflammation; implications for intradiscal therapy. J Orthop Res 37(11): 2445-2456.
4. Cheung KM et al. (1976). Prevalence and pattern of lumbar magnetic resonance imaging changes in a population study of one thousand forty-three individuals. Spine 34(9): 934-40.
5. De Kunder SL, et al. (2018). Lumbar Interbody Fusion: A Historical Overview and a Future Perspective. Spine43(16): 1161-1168.
6. Golob AL, & Wipf JE. (2014). Low back pain. Med Clin North Am 98: 405–42

7. Han C, et al. (2015). Differentiation of transforming growth factor β1-induced mesenchymal stem cells into nucleus pulposus-like cells under simulated microgravity conditions. Cell Mol Biol 61(2): 50-55.
8. Hartvigsen J, et al. (2018). What low back pain is and why we need to pay attention. Lancet 391(10137): 2356-2367.
9. Horst TC, et al. (2020). Mesenchymal Stem Cells. In: essential Current Concepts in Stem Cell Biol. Springer Nature, 21-3
10. Hoy D, et al. (2012) A systematic review of the global prevalence of low back pain. Arthritis Rheum 64(6): 2028-37.
11. Jin ES, et al. (2013). Analysis of molecular expression in adipose tissue-derived mesenchymal stem cells: prospects for use in the treatment of intervertebral disc degeneration. J Korean Neurosurg Soc 53(4): 207–212.
12. Gugjoo MB. (2022). Mesenchymal Stem Cells Therapeutic Applications in Central Nervous System Disorders. In: Therapeutic Applications of Mesenchymal Stem Cells in Veterinary Medicine. Springer Nature. pp. 163-212.
13. Gugjoo MB. (2019). Mesenchymal stem cell Basic research and applications in dog medicine. J Cell Physiol234(10): 16779-16811.
14. Katz JN. (2006). Lumbar disc disorders and low-back pain: Socioeconomic factors and consequences. J Bone Jt Surg Am 88(Suppl 2): 21-4.
15. Kim HS, et al. (2020). Incidental durotomy during endoscopic stenosis lumbar decompression: inci- dence, classification, and proposed management strategies. World Neurosurg 139: e13-e22.
16. Le Maitre CL, et al. (2009). An in vitro study investigating the survival and phenotype of mesenchymal stem cells following injection into nucleus pulposus tissue. Arthritis Res Ther 11(1): R20.
17. May RD, et al. (2019). Application of Cytokines of the Bone Morphogenetic Protein (BMP) Family in Spinal Fusion—Effects on the Bone, Intervertebral Disc and Mesenchymal Stromal Cells. Curr Stem Cell Res Ther 14(8): 618-643.
18. Pan M, et al. (2020). Percutaneous endo- scopic lumbar discectomy: indications and complications. Pain Physician 23(1): 49-56.
19. Qi L, et al. (2019). Umbilical cord mesenchymal stem cell conditioned medium restored the expression of collagen II and aggrecan in nucleus pulposus mesenchymal stem cells exposed to high glucose. J Bone Miner Metab 37(3): 455-466.

20. Richardson SM, et al. (2006). Intervertebral disc cell-mediated mesenchymal stem cell differentiation. Stem Cells. 24(3): 707-16.
21. Roughley PJ. (2004). Biology of intervertebral disc aging and degeneration: involvement of the extracellular matrix. Spine 29(23): 2691-9
22. Sakai D, et al. (2005). Differentiation of mesenchymal stem cells transplanted to a rabbit degenerative disc model: potential and limitations for stem cell therapy in disc regeneration. Spine 30(21): 2379-87.
23. Vadalà G, et al. (2008). Coculture of bone marrow mesenchymal stem cells and nucleus pulposus cells modulate gene expression profile without cell fusion. Spine 33(8): 870-6.
24. Vickers L, et al. (2018). Mesenchymal stem cell therapies for intervertebral disc degeneration: Consideration of the degenerate niche, Spine 2(2): e1055.
25. Xu J, et al. (2016). BMP enhances the effect of BMSCs on extracellular matrix remodelling in a rabbit model of intervertebral disc degeneration. Febs J 283(9): 1689-700.
26. Zhan J, et al. (2018). Fasudil promotes BMSC migration via activating the MAPK signalling pathway and application in a model of spinal cord injury. Stem CellsInt. 2018: 9793845.
27. Zhang W, et al. (2022). Application of stem cells in the repair of intervertebral disc degeneration, Stem Cell Res Therapy13(1): 70.
28. Zhou X, et al. (2015). BMP3 alone and together with TGF-β promote the differentiation of human mesenchymal stem cells into a nucleus pulposus-like phenotype. Int J Mol Sci 16(9): 20344-59.

CHAPTER TEN

Mesenchymal Stem Cells for Combating Cancer

Mir Bilal Ahmad and **Ather ul Islam**
Department of Biochemistry, University of Kashmir, Hazratbal, Srinagar, J&K, India

Abstract

Mesenchymal Stem Cells (MSCs) possess some important properties that are exploited by researchers to combat various diseases including cancer. Promising results have been obtained where it has been shown that MSCs play a key role in suppressing angiogenesis besides regulating other aspects of tumor growth. Whereas MSCs are primarily involved in inhibiting tumor growth, certain studies also highlight the pro-cancerous effect of MSCs. Therefore a sustained effort and extensive research is needed to understand the interplay between MSCs and tumor cells to get better know-how of MSCs and their working mechanism. Here we provide an insight about MSCs and their role in delivering anti-cancerous compounds to the target tissues and future aspects related with MSC based therapeutics.

Keywords: mesenchymal stem cells, cancer, therapeutics, angiogenesis, apoptosis, cell signaling, exosomes.

Introduction

Mesenchymal Stem Cells (MSCs) are adult stem cells which were originally found in bone marrow (Friedenstein, 1976) but later in other tissues like placenta, umbilical cord, peripheral blood, adipose tissue and hair follicles (da Silva Meirelles et al., 2006). MSCs are also called as mesenchymal stromal cells and have some important characteristics like multi-lineage differentiation, immunoevasiveness, immune-modulatory and self-renewal (Jiang et al., 2002). To be specified as MSC, a cell must exhibit minimum three characteristics put forward by International Society for

Cellular Therapy (ISCT). These include I) plastic adherence (when grown in-vitro), ii) expression of certain positive surface antigens like CD90, CD105, CD73 and negative surface markers like CD14, CD34, CD45, CD19 and HLA DR and iii) differentiate into mesodermal cell lineage i.e. adipocytes, chondrocytes and osteoblasts when grown in different culture media.

Owing to their advantages, MSCs have become widely used stem cell types in clinical applications and have shown promising results in combating various diseases like cardiac ischemia, neurological disorders, diabetes, bone and cartilage diseases. Recent research also reflects the role of MSCs in cancer therapy (Wei et al., 2013). Below we present an overview about MSCs and their therapeutic role in cancer treatment (**Fig. 10.1**).

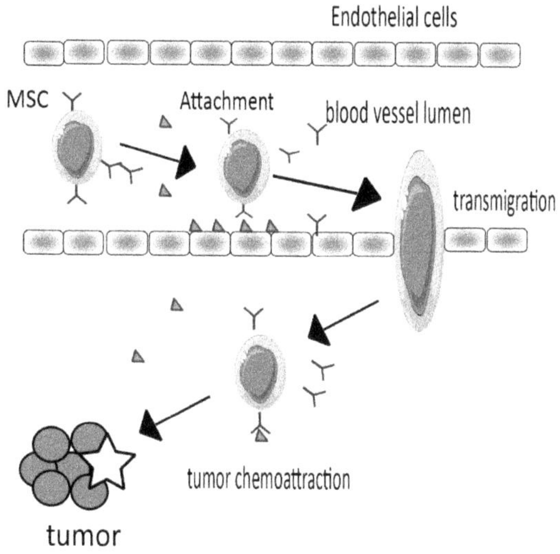

Fig. 10.1: Chemo-attractant induced migration of MSCs towards the tumor lesion

Role of MSCs in combating cancer

Recent studies have shown that MSCs spontaneously reach to the inflamed or damaged tissue as well as to the primary and the malignant tumor masses (Ullah et al., 2019). Although mobilization of MSCs to tumor microenvironment is primarily carried out by CXXL12/CXCR4 signalling pathway (Gao et al., 2009; Xu et al., 2009), however, other factors like TGFβ1, PDGF (platelet derived growth factor), MMP2 (Matrix Metallo proteinase 2), IL8 (interleukin 8) also play a vital role in MSCs migration (Nakamizo et al., 2005; Birnbaum et al., 2007; Bhoopathi et al., 2011).

Many of the cancers arise because of the mutation or dysregulated functioning of p21 which plays an important role in cell cycle regulation by blocking G1/S transition. It has been shown that MSCs in hepatocytes up-regulate the expression of p21 (both in-vitro and in-vivo) thus arresting cell cycle (Lu et al., 2008). Besides, MSCs are shown to trigger apoptosis in cancer cells by inducing expression of caspase 3 and caspase 9 proteins (Dasari et al., 2010). MSCs also release cytotoxic agents like TRAIL (TNF Related Apoptosis Inducing Ligand) that promotes apoptosis in various types of cancers (Wiley et al., 1995). Recent work also showers light on the role of bone marrow MSCs in promoting apoptosis of U251 glioma cells. BM-MSCs target PI3K/AKT pathway and down regulate the expression of these proteins (Lu et al., 2019). A recent study showed that BM-MSCs suppress vascular growth in Gli36 glioma xneograft by downregulating PDGF/PDGFR pathway (Lu et al., 2019). Additionally, naïve MSCs also suppress tumor formation by inhibiting Wnt-signalling pathway courtesy modulation of DKK1 protein released by tumor cells. Cyclin D2 and c-Myc are also down-regulated in these cells leading to cell-cycle arrest and thus tumor suppression (Lu et al., 2008; Qiao et al., 2008; Zhu et al., 2009). In addition to signaling molecules and cyclin/CDKs, angiogenesis also plays a vital role in the development of cancer by supplying nutrients to the rapidly dividing cells thus potentially making it a good candidate for therapeutic intervention. A large number of studies have shown that vascular endothelial growth factor A (VEGF- A) acts as inducer of angiogenesis. The VEGF-A gene whose expression is regulated by oncogene signaling and hypoxia (Ferrara et al. 2010) codes for a ligand that is involved in formation of new blood vessels. MSCs have the potential to carry anti angiogenic substances to restrict the tumor growth and metastasis. Treatment of tumor cells with MSC derived exosomes containing miR-16 downregulate the expression of VEGF thus suppressing angiogenesis (Lee et al., 2013). Targeted delivery of exosomes containing miRNAs thus pave a way to control the expression/suppression of certain genes involved in angiogenesis and tumor growth.

MSCs as carriers of anti-cancer therapeutics

Over the past years, researchers have worked hard over stem cells to get these deliver anti-cancerous therapeutics to target tissue. In this backdrop, mesenchymal stem cells (MSCs) have got much attention as possible therapeutic carriers due to their inherent characteristic to migrate towards tumor sites. Genetic engineering plays a vital and fundamental role in helping these MSCs deliver therapeutics to target tissue. Studies show that MSCs derived from human umbilical cord transduced with adenoviral vectors and expressing IFNβ substantially inhibit the growth of breast cancer cells via apoptotic induction (Shen et al., 2016). Nanotechnology is employed as an interesting experiment to produce human MSCs expressing suicide protein TRAIL for targeting and eliminating glioma cells in mice (Jiang et al., 2016). Oncolytic viruses are loaded into MSCs to get these used as anti-tumor therapeutics. Oncolytic adenoVirus (ICOVIR5) infected MSCs provide therapeutic benefit to the mice suffering from lung carcinoma via mobilization of T-cells and subsequent inhibition of tumor growth (Rincon et al., 2017). Another strategy used to arm MSCs is loading of anti-cancer drugs and then effectively using them to deliver anti-cancer drugs to tumor sites. For example, MSCs loaded with *doxorubicin* are effective against mice thyroid carcinoma, breast cancer and oral squamous carcinoma (Coccè et al., 2017; Kalimuthu et al., 2018). Similarly, MSCs loaded with *paclitaxel* are effective against brain, metastatic lung cancer, mesothelioma, leukemia and pancreatic cancer (Pessina et al., 2013; Pessina et al., 2015; Brini et al., 2016 Bonomi et al., 2017; Petrella et al., 2017). Taken together, MSCs offer a ray of hope for researchers to effectively tackle the unrestricted growth of tumor cells by acting at multiple targets.

Limitations of MSCs as cancer therapeutics

Although MSCs offer a promising treatment option for combating cancer yet a number of issues hamper their extensive usage like proper homing and survival of graft after its implantation. Additionally the survival of delivered MSCs at the target site also pose a limitation to its usage.

Conclusion and future perspective

Owing to the ability of Mesenchymal Stem Cells to home to damaged tissues, getting differentiated into various cell types, self-renewal, immunoevasiveness, these are widely used in treatment of large number of diseases. However, the extensive therapeutic-usage of MSC in treatment of cancer is hampered because of both pro-tumor and anti-tumor effects in pre-clinical trials. Despite these all odds, latest MSCs offer a ray of hope to cancer patients by delivering anti-cancer treatments in a personalized way. Next challenge for MSC based therapeutics is to better understand the interplay and mechanism between MSCs and target tissues. This would explore new areas and new dimensions which in turn would help the researchers deal with cancer both effectively and efficiently. Additionally, the introduction of MSC-derived extracellular vesicles as cell-free therapy has not only fetched positive results but has also evaded the safety concerns associated with the use of live cells. Moreover, exosomes released by MSCs can be engineered in a better way to get more promising results related to MSC based therapeutics. Molecular based approach towards MSCs can also prove beneficial. Introduction of pro-apoptotic genes, upregulating anti-cancer related genes may dilute the pro-tumor effect of MSC based therapeutics and thus help the society in a better way. Altogether, MSCs offer a better choice as therapeutic tool but a lot more needs to be explored to make them prime choice for cancer treatment.

References:

1. Bhoopathi P, et al. (2011). MMP-2 mediates mesenchymal stem cell tropism towards medulloblastoma tumors. Gene Ther 18: 692–701.
2. Birnbaum T, et al. (2007). Malignant gliomas actively recruit bone marrow stromal cells by secreting angiogenic cytokines. J Neurooncol 83: 241–247.
3. Bonomi A, et al. (2017). Effect of canine mesenchymal stromal cells loaded with paclitaxel on growth of canine glioma and human glioblastoma cell lines. Vet J 223: 41-47
4. Brini AT, et al. (2016). Cell-mediated drug delivery by gingival interdental papilla mesenchymal stromal cells (GinPa-MSCs) loaded with paclitaxel. Expert Opin Drug Deliv13: 789-798.
5. Coccè V, et al. (2017). Drug Loaded Gingival Mesenchymal Stromal Cells (GinPa-MSCs) Inhibit In Vitro Proliferation of Oral Squamous Cell Carcinoma. Sci Rep7: 9376.
6. da Silva Meirelles L, et al. (2006). Mesenchymal stem cells reside in virtually all post-natal organs and tissues. J Cell Sci 119: 2204–2213.
7. Dasari VR, et al. (2010). Cord blood stem cell-mediated induction of apoptosis in glioma downregulates X-linked inhibitor of apoptosis protein (XIAP). PLoS One5: e11813.
8. Ferrara N. (2010). Pathways mediating VEGF-independent tumor angiogenesis. Cytokine Growth Factor Rev 21: 21–26.

9. Friedenstein AJ, et al. (1970). The development of fibroblast colonies in monolayer cultures of guinea-pig bone marrow and spleen cells. Cell Tissue Kinet 3: 393–403.
10. Gao H, et al. (2009). Activation of signal transducers and activators of transcription 3 and focal adhesion kinase by stromal cell-derived factor 1 is required for migration of human mesenchymal stem cells in response to tumor cell-conditioned medium. Stem Cells 27: 857–865.
11. Hao C, et al. (2001). Induction and intracellular regulation of tumor necrosis factor-related apoptosis-inducing ligand (TRAIL) mediated apotosis in human malignant glioma cells. Cancer Res 61: 1162–1170.
12. Jiang X, et al. (2016). Nanoparticle engineered TRAIL-overexpressing adipose-derived stem cells target and eradicate glioblastoma via intracranial delivery. Proc Natl Acad Sci USA 113: 13857–13862.
13. Jiang Y, et al. (2002). Pluripotency of mesenchymal stem cells derived from adult marrow. Nature 418: 41–49.
14. Kalimuthu S, et al. (2018). Migration of mesenchymal stem cells to tumor xenograft models and *in vitro* drug delivery by doxorubicin. Int J Med Sci 15: 1051-1061.
15. Lee J-K, et al. (2013). Exosomes derived from mesenchymal stem cells suppress angiogenesis by down-regulating VEGF expression in breast cancer cells. PLoS ONE 8(12): e84256.
16. Lu L, et al. (2019). Bone marrow mesenchymal stem cells suppress growth and promote the apoptosis of glioma U251 cells through downregulation of the PI3K/AKT signaling pathway. Biomed Pharmacother 112: 108625.
17. Lu Y-R, et al. (2008). The growth inhibitory effect of mesenchymal stem cells on tumor cells in vitro and in vivo. Cancer Biol Ther 7(2): 245–51.
18. Lu YR, et al. (2008). The growth inhibitory effect of mesenchymal stem cells on tumor cells in vitroand in vivo. Cancer Biol Ther7: 245-251.
19. Nakamizo A, et al. (2005). Human bone marrow-derived mesenchymal stem cells in the treatment of gliomas. Cancer Res 65: 3307–3318.
20. Pessina A, et al. (2013). Mesenchymal stromal cells primed with Paclitaxel attract and kill leukaemia cells, inhibit angiogenesis and improve survival of leukaemia-bearing mice. Br J Haematol160: 766-778
21. Pessina A, et al. (2015). Drug-releasing mesenchymal cells strongly suppress B16 lung metastasis in a syngeneic murine model. J Exp Clin Cancer Res 34: 82

22. Petrella F, et al. (2017). Paclitaxel-releasing mesenchymal stromal cells inhibit in vitroproliferation of human mesothelioma cells. Biomed Pharmacother87: 755-758.
23. Qiao L, et al. (2008). Dkk-1 secreted by mesenchymal stem cells inhibits growth of breast cancer cells via depression of Wnt signalling. Cancer Lett 269(1): 67–77.
24. Rincon E, et al. (2017). Mesenchymal stem cell carriers enhance antitumor efficacy of oncolytic adenoviruses in an immunocompetent mouse model. Oncotarget 8: 45415–45431.
25. Shen CJ, et al. (2016). Human umbilical cord matrix-derived stem cells expressing interferonbeta gene inhibit breast cancer cells via apoptosis. Oncotarget 7: 34172–34179.
26. Ullah M, et al. (2019). Mesenchymal Stromal Cell Homing: Mechanisms and Strategies for Improvement. Science15: 421-438
27. Wei Y, et al. (2013). Mesenchymal stem cells: A new trend for cell therapy. Acta Pharmacol Sin 34(6): 747.
28. Wiley SR, et al. (1995). Identification and characterization of a new member of the TNF family that induces apoptosis. Immunity 3: 673–682.
29. Xu WT, et al. (2009). Human mesenchymal stem cells (hMSCs) target osteosarcoma and promote its growth and pulmonary metastasis. Cancer Lett 281: 32–41.
30. Zhu Y, et al. (2009). Human mesenchymal stem cells inhibit cancer cell proliferation by secreting DKK-1. Leukemia 23(5): 925.

CHAPTER ELEVEN

Mesenchymal Stem Cells for Chronic Renal Failure

Manish Arya[1], **Aditya D. Deshpande**[2], **Sharun Khan**[1]and **Mudasir B Gugjoo**[3]

[1]Divison of Surgery, [2]Divison of Physiology & Climatology, ICAR-IVRI, Bareilly, UP, India

[3]Veterinary Clinical Complex, FVSc & AH, SKUAST-K, Shuhama, J&K, India

Abstract

Chronic renal failure poses a great challenge for clinicians as there is no definitive therapeutics for the condition. The condition is being treated symptomatically without actual renal tissue regeneration. In order to actually treat the condition, tissue engineering is being evaluated. Mesenchymal stem cells make an important component of the tissue engineering. The cells have ability to secrete plethora of pro-healing and regenerating factors that can bring tissue regeneration. Although there is lack of specific literature that can demonstrate such a potential of the MSCs however, numerous in vitro and in vivo studies show positive outcomes, although short of the regeneration. The current chapter shall focus of MSCs potential therapeutic role in chronic renal failure.

Key words: Chronic renal failure; mesenchymal stem cells; regeneration; renoprotection

Introduction

The kidney is an important part of urinary system in body as it helps in the excretion of waste products and re-absorption of important nutrients from urine. Besides, it also helps in maintaining normal blood pressure by secreting the hormone erythropoietin. Ingestion of toxic food, nephrotoxic drugs, infection, ischemia, etc. may cause insult to the parenchyma of the renal capsule or parenchyma, causing an increase in intratubular pressure of the kidney due to obstruction caused by dead cells leading to abrupt changes in the functioning of kidney, i.e., acute renal failure (Morigi et al., 2004) or progressive necrosis and finally death of renal cells over a period leading to degenerative structural changes and thus halting the functioning of kidney, i.e., chronic renal failure.

Generally, treatment of renal failure follows control in the injury of renal parenchyma or progression of damage by removal of the causative agent, proliferation of renal tubular cells, etc (Rookmaaker et al., 2004). For this, various methods such as medical management, including the use of Dopamine, furosemide, mannitol, calcium channel blockers, atrial natriuretic peptide, and several other hormonal or pharmacologic substances (Grino, 1994), kidney transplantation, or renal dialysis is generally employed, but none of them provide long lasting and satisfactory results.

Now-a-days, there has been increased interest in using stem cells in therapeutics and regenerative medicine. Mesenchymal stem cells are specialized endogenous cells with the ability to repair injury of the host due to different properties such as self-renewal, multiplication, differentiation, immunomodulation, antibacterial (Gugjoo et al., 2020), and little teratogenic effects (Cardoso et al., 2017). These cells are easy to isolate from various resources such as bone marrow, adipose tissue, dental pulp, embryonic tissue, endometrium, gingiva, hair follicle, lungs, limbal epithelium, muscle, ovary, periodontal ligament, peripheral blood, periosteum, synovial fluid and membrane, umbilical cord, Wharton's Jelly, etc. lack of ethical issues, etc. Mesenchymal cells show the expression of several surface markers such as CD44, CD73, CD90, CD105, CD166, CD271, and Stro-1, without CD14, CD34, CD45, and HLA-DR. These cells are plastic adherent and are able to differentiate into trilineage (Peired et al., 2016).

Potential mechanisms of mesenchymal stem cells in chronic renal failure

Mesenchymal cells may prove reno-protective, i.e., they might be able to generate renal tubules by various mechanisms, such as the release of paracrine signals and initiating mechanisms for the repair of local tissue, etc. (Du & Zhu, 2014; Gugjoo, 2022). The studies on urinary regenerative medicine utilzing MSCs encompasses small ruminants and pets.

Ischemia injuries to the proximal tubule decrease perfusion in renal failure leading to deposition of lipid peroxidation products and free radicals due to an inactive antioxidant system. This causes damage to renal tubules leading to inflammatory changes and, ultimately, cell and parenchymal degeneration (Ozkok & Edelstein, 2014). In a renal injury mouse model MSCs (1×10^6 cells) were injected intravenously. The cells engrafted with signs of the fusion into parenchymal cells, and thus can potentially repair kidney (Choi et al., 2009). Intra-renal cellular infusion leads to complete renal engraftment but has anaesthetic risk while intravenous injection might avert such a risk but requires higher doses as the majority of the cells usually end up in lung or liver localization (Vidane et al. 2016). Renal arterial injection via femoral or carotid artery appears feasible and safe within a 3-month postoperative period (Thomson et al. 2019).

The renal degenrating cells elicit release of various chemical mediators which enhances arrival of mesenchymal cells at damages site (homing) and differentiation into renal cells (Ullah et al., 2019). However, the population of these cells may not be sufficient enough to cover the required pro-healing effects. Thus, additional MSCs might be able to sufficiently immunomodulate locally by releasing various chemicals and reduce cell apoptosis, restore the mechanism of inducing prosurvival genes, and down-regulate pro-apoptotic genes. Factors released include vascular endothelial growth factor, stromal cell-derived factor-1, fibroblast growth factor, insulin-like growth factor (IGF), keratinocyte growth factor, hepatocyte growth factor, and monocyte chemoattractant protein-1. Besides, MSCs help expand T-cells to a regulatory phenotype, converting macrophages to anti-inflammatory and immunosuppressive M2 phenotypes and inhibiting antigen-presenting cells (Makhlough et al., 2017) and dendritic cell maturation (Erpicum, 2014).

MSCs additionally release extracellular vesicles, which act as antioxidants, anti-cell apoptosis, and anti-inflammatory agents. These vesicles also help regulate neo-vascularization, cell cycle, proliferation, etc (Huang & Yang, 2021). BM-MSCs are safe to be administered in seven patients suffering from chronic renal failure with an 18-month follow-up (Makhlough et al., 2021). In a murine model (cis-platin-induced acute renal injury), MSCs were renoprotective in nature. MSCs showed engraftment and differentiated into tubular structures (Morigi et al., 2004). Other study that transplanted human-derived Wharton-Jelly mesenchymal stromal cells on renal ischemia-reperfusion injury in rats. Showed their anti-apoptosis properties with an ability to reduce levels of free radicals in the kidney (Zhang et al., 2014). The absence of MHC-II and T-cell co-stimulation property make mesenchymal cells easier to transplant from allogenic or xenogenic resources (Gugjoo et al., 2020).

Conclusion

Chronic kidney diseases have a complex pathophysiology that may involve both ischemic/inflammatory and immunological injury. In contrast to most current pharmacological agents that target only a single pathophysiological pathway, cell-based therapies such as MSC act through multiple mechanisms and have the potential to target immunological, vascular, and inflammatory pathways. In addition, MSC can engraft and survive long-term in the specific target tissue and are nonimmunogenic and immunosuppressive. This has important implications for the therapeutic application of MSC in tissue repair and regeneration, in that MSC derived from healthy unrelated volunteer donors can be cryopreserved, thus making them available promptly for patients in a variety of acute and chronic clinical settings. The clinical application of MSC is broad and has generated significant interest in clinicians from diverse fields, with preclinical and clinical data in various conditions, including osteogenesis imperfecta, osteoarthritis, and cardiac regeneration. MSCs are currently being used in haematopoietic stem cell transplantation, and although numbers to date are small, the results in high-risk populations with severe graft versus host disease are encouraging. However, many questions remain about their basic biology and long-term safety. More research is needed to understand these cells physiological role, their migration stimuli, and the pathways that mediate their apparent beneficial effects in regeneration and repair. Protocols that limit the differentiation potential of the cells into a specific lineage when used for the treatment of a specific disease are needed, along with studies that determine the correct dose, schedule, and administration route. Despite the lack of apparent adverse effects seen in trials to date, longer-term follow-up is required, given the possibility of malignant transformation. Finally, this basic research needs to be translated into functional experiments in animal models of renal damage in order to clarify the therapeutic potential of a stem cell approach.

References

1. Cardoso MT, et al. (2017). Characterization of teratogenic potential and gene expression in canine and feline amniotic membrane derived stem cells. Reprod Domest Anim 52(Suppl. 2): 58- 64

2. Choi S. (2009). The role of mesenchymal stem cells in the functional improvement of chronic renal failure. Stem cells Dev 18(3): 521-530.
3. Du T, & Zhu YJ. (2014). The regulation of inflammatory mediators in acute kidney injury via exogenous mesenchymal stem cells. Mediators Inflamm 2014: 261697.
4. Erpicum P, et al. (2014). Mesenchymal stromal cell therapy in conditions of renal ischaemia/reperfusion. Nephrol Dialysis Transplant 29(8):1487-93
5. Grino JM. (1994). A platelet activating factor antagonist for preventing post-transplant renal failure. A double-blind, randomized study. Study Group in Renal Transplantation. Ann Intern Med121: 345–347
6. Gugjoo MB. (2022). Mesenchymal Stem Cells Therapeutic Applications in Urinary System Disorders. In: Therapeutic Applications of Mesenchymal Stem Cells in Veterinary Medicine. Springer Nature. pp. 324-340.
7. Gugjoo MB, & Amarpal (2018). Mesenchymal stem cell research in sheep: Current status and future prospects. Small Rumin Res 169: 46-56
8. Gugjoo MB, et al. (2020). Mesenchymal stem cell-mediated immuno-modulatory and anti-inflammatory mechanisms in immune and allergic disorders. Recent Patents on Inflammat Allergy Drug Disc 14(1): 3-14.
9. Huang Y, & Yang L. (2021). Mesenchymal stem cells and extracellular vesicles in therapy against kidney diseases. Stem Cell Res & Therapy 12(1): 1-12.
10. Makhlough A, et al. (2018). Bone marrow–mesenchymal stromal cell infusion in patients with chronic kidney disease: A safety study with 18 months of follow-up. Cytotherapy 20(5): 660-669.
11. Morigi M, et al. (2004). Mesenchymal stem cells are renotropic, helping to repair the kidney and improve function in acute renal failure. J Am Soc Nephrol 15(7): 1794-1804.
12. Ozkok A, & Edelstein CL. (2014). Pathophysiology of cisplatin-induced acute kidney injury. Biomed Res Int 2014: 967826.
13. Rookmaaker MB, et al. (2004). Progenitor cells in the kidney: biology and therapeutic prospectives. Kidney Int 66: 518–522.
14. Thomson AL, et al. (2019). Intra-arterial renal infusion of autologous mesenchymal stem cells for treatment of chronic kidney disease in cats: Phase I clinical trial. J Vet Intern Med 2019; 1–9.
15. Ullah M, et al. (2019). Mesenchymal stromal cell homing: mechanisms and strategies for improvement. Science 15: 421-38.

16. Vidane AS, et al. (2016) Transplantation of amniotic membrane-derived multipotent cells ameliorates and delays the progression of chronic kidney disease in cats. Reprod Domest Anim 51(Suppl. 3):1–11.
17. Zhang G, et al. (2014). The anti-oxidative role of micro-vesicles derived from human Wharton-Jelly mesenchymal stromal cells through NOX2/gp91 (phox) suppression in alleviating renal ischemia-reperfusion injury in rats. PloS One, 9(3): e92129.
18. Zuk P, et al. (2001). Multilineage cells from human adipose tissue: Implications for cell-based therapies. Tissue Eng 7(2): 211-28.

CHAPTER TWELVE

Mesenchymal Stem Cells for Alzheimer's Disease

Kamran Nissar [1,2,3] and **Parveena Firdous** [1,4]

[1]*Centre of Research for Development*, [2]*Department of Clinical Biochemistry*, [4]*Department of Zoology, University of Kashmir, Hazratbal, Srinagar, J&K, India*

[3]*Institute of Mental Health and Neurosciences, Srinagar*

Abstract

Alzheimer's disease (AD) is the commonest form dementia. It is a neurodegenerative disorder, generally affecting elderly people above the age group of 60-65 years. Although the exact etiology of the disease is not known, but there are number factors that have been found to be associated with AD development or progression-like age, gene polymorphism, diet, physical inactivity, stress, social isolation, familial history of AD, head trauma, neuronal inflammation etc. Alzheimer's disease affects approximately 48 million people worldwide. Alzheimer's disease (AD) is not usual aging process, but a complicated medical condition ultimately usurping not just life of patient but its caregivers both physically and mentally, and economically as well. The frequency of the disease is expected to double by 2030 and triple by the year 2050. As of now number of approaches were tried for the cure of Alzheimer's disease, but no approach proved to be beneficial up to the mark, even though present medication help improved quality of patient life to some extent. Now scientists are looking for Mesenchymal Stem Cell therapy, as the approach has shown some remarkable results in animal models. Hence, the importance of a multidisciplinary approach for understanding, prevention, cure and management of AD is the need of hour.

Key words: Alzhiemer's disease; Model; Pathology

Introduction

Alzheimer disease (AD) is a multi-factorial condition wherein both genetic as well as environmental factors are responsible for pathogenesis. It has been agreed upon by many epidemiological studies that different demographic factors-like age, sex, race and social class play role in AD pathology, but age is one among the key significant risk factors for cognitive decline (Doruk et al., 2010) and Alzheimer's disease (Herrup et al., 2010). With advancement of age, chances of AD increase to 19% in people of 75-84 years of age (Knopman et al., 2001) and in the age group above 85 years prevalence of AD is 30-35% which may go upto 50% (Ferri et al., 2005). Pathological changes that have been identified in AD are similar to the changes found in normal aged brain, but there is more severity in pathological changes found in it (Reisberg, 1983; Rossor and Mountjoy, 1986). Therefore, reduction in brain volume, synapse loss, dendrite loss, increase in ventricular spaces and reduction in weight of brain, accompanied by senile plaques and neurofibrillary tangles, have been reported in cognitively normal brain (Imhof et al., 2007). Besides, even after post-mortem, it was impossible to differentiate early stage Alzheimer's dementia from normal aging (Mann et al., 1987). AD can be easily misunderstood as normal age related complication, which include forgetfulness, confusion, misplacing things, mood swings etc. But AD is not usual aging process, but a complicated medical condition ultimately usurping not just life of patient but its caregivers both physically and mentally, and economically as well.

AD significantly increases the burden of healthcare costs and have a significant effect on the quality of life (QoL) of patient as well as caregiver(s). After cancer and coronary heart disease, the disease ranks third costlier disease (Meek et al.,1998) with an average annual cost of whopping 80-100 billion US$ in US alone (CDC and NCCDPHP, 2000).

Alzheimer disease pathogenesis

Till date, the exact cause of AD is not fully elucidated, but Amyloid cascade hypothesis is widely accepted in explaining the genesis and progression of the disease. Now the studies are indicating that this hypothesis doesn't fully explain the mechanism of AD pathology (Mengtian Guo et al., 2020). Now, mitochondrial cascade hypothesis, tau hypothesis and neuroinflammation hypothesis are being proposed successively (Shen Y et al., 2018; Fevrier B et al., 2004). Even though amyloid plaques are still strong candidates, and considered to be hallmark feature of the AD. According to Amyloid cascade hypothesis one of the hallmarks of aging is change in proteostasis (Witkowski et al., 2017). The amyloidogenic breakdown of APP (amyloid precursor protein), results in the formation of fibrils, that gets deposited extraneuronally leading to death of neurons and formation of senile plaques (Bolós et al., 2017). An AD phenotype as well as Aβ plaques, neurofibrillary tangles and gliosis result in mice with dsRNA analog, because of systemic immune challenge in mice, indicating that immune challenge(s) can initiate the condition (Krstic et al., 2012). In case of AD neuroinflammation is initiated by neurofibrillary tangles (NFTs) and Aβ-plaques. The AD progression occurs with the activation of PRRs (protein recognition receptors), Aβ-plaques and NFTs (neurofibrillary tangles) that provides differential and distinct signaling patterns to the concerned cells. This whole incident eventually directs to NLRP3 inflammasome assembly, and NFkB reliant proinflammatory gene transcription that proceeds to generation of pro-inflammatory cytokines (Latz et al., 2013; Liu et al., 2017). Chronic inflammation adds to the stress of brain cells, which are already weakened by aging. The events ultimately leads to neuronal death, thus Alzheimer's disease (Gugjoo, 2022).

Mesenchymal Stem Cells Therapy for Alzheimer's disease

Stem Cells (MSCs) are the undifferentiated cells that have the marvellous characters-like self renewal, can proliferate from a single cell, differentiate into different cell types, evades immune system etc. On the basis of origin, stem cells can be grouped into (I) embryonic stem cells (ESCs); (II) induced pluripotent stem cells (iPSCs); (III) fetal stem cells; and (IV) adult stem cells. Mesenchymal stem cells (MSCs) are adult stem cells, which are readily available in bone marrow, bone, peripheral blood, adipose tissue, umblical cord blood and Wharton's jelly (Kolios et al., 2013). As we are well aware, that cells do express different markers called cluster of differentiation (CD), which help in differentiating one cell type from other. Similarly, a cell expressing CD90, CD73, CD105 and CD44, while not expressing CD45 and CD31 is referred to as MSC. The basic and normal functioning of MSCs is reparative process i.e migration to injury site and taking part in repair process (Staff et al., 2019). The cells boost repairing of tissues by reducing apoptosis and enhancing angiogenesis (Cooney et al., 2016). MSCs have strong potential of differentiation into different lineages as: neuronal cells, osteocytes, chondrocytes, or adipocytes after being stimulated by specific growth factors (Kim et al., 2020).

As we know, that amyloid plaques, tau proteins, and finally inflammation make the characteristic features of AD in brain, and to our surprise and probably good luck MSCs have the ability to counter all the said features to a very large extent. In scientifically developed AD models, decrease in Aβ plaque load, β-secretase and hyperphosphorylation of tau, as well as microglial inflammation reversal, and stimulatory effect for cytokines which are anti-inflammatory in nature, are some of the versatile properties of MSCs gives MSCs strong candidature for being considered as therapeutic agents. MSCs have been found to downregulate pro-inflammatory cytokines, thus have anti-inflammatory effect (Liu et al., 2020). MSCs secrete certain neurotrophic factors (stimulate neurogenesis and synaptogenesis), overexpress neuroprotective cytokines (IL-10) while simultaneosuly reduce secretion of proinflammatory factors (TNF-α, and IL-1β). These cells can enhance phagocytic properties of microglial cells, improve neovascularization, overcome Aβ plaque and tau induce cell death and additionally alter autophagic pathways (Alipour et al., 2019).

Furthermore, studies have shown that BM-MSCs administration ameliorates diabetes-induced cognitive deficit by transferring exosomes from these MSCs into astrocytes (Masako K et al., 2020). In AD mice model, amelioration of inflammation and synaptogenesis are reported after injecting BM-MSCs intracerebroventrically. Astrocytes are the basic cells for synaptogenesis, therefore, restoration of astrocytic function may have led to synaptogenesis, and hence improvement in cognition deficit (Masako et al., 2020). Basically, MSCs inhibit astrogliosis but promote non-reactive astrocytes (Cong liu et al., 2022).

The MSC treatment is a novel method for treating AD that involves the systemic introduction of MSCs into the patient's body. MSCs therapy in Alzheimer's disease focuses on replacing damaged cells with healthy stem cells that grow on their own, and differentiate into healthy brain cells (van der Kant et al., 2020). Alzheimer's stem cell therapy aims to improve memory, neuronal regeneration, and finally Patient recovery through replacement of damaged brain cells with healthy ones. MSCs, once transplanted, can improve functional recovery, promote survival and improve metabolic activity, potentially aiding in the recovery from AD. Furthermore, in AD mouse models, MSC therapy has the potential to reduce Aβ deposition and thus improve AD pathology (Choi et al., 2014). As a result, the most exciting aspect of MSC therapy for AD treatment is the possibility of completely stopping disease progression while also regenerating damaged neurons, although it remaisn to be proved.

Proposed mechanism of MSC therapy in the treatment of Alzheimer's disease

Several mechanisms were proposed to explain the pathway (Figure 1) utilized by MSCs in treatment of Alzheimer's disease. The main mechanism of action (of MSCs) in Alzheimer's disease treatment has long been thought to be "cell replacement". However, mounting evidences suggest that transplanted MSCs can only survive for a limited period in the host, get intravenously trapped in the spleen and lungs (Park BN et al., 2018; Kim et al.., 2020; Park et al., 2020). Currently, it is widely assumed that transplanted MSCs primarily function via paracrine effects (Kim et al., 2020; Liu et al., 2021). Through paracrine action, mesenchymal cells secrete a large number of angiogenic and neurotrophic factors, including GDNF (Glial cell derived neurotrophic factor), VEGF (vascular endothelial growth factor), BDNF (brain-derived neurotrophic factor), and IGF (insulin growth factor), among others. These angiogenic and neurogenic factors in the diseased area may improve the microenvironment for the remaining neurons, promoting neural repair and regeneration. Santamaria et al., (2021) proved, persistent memory recovery as well as a reduction in amyloid plaque load and reactive gliosis in the APP/PS1 AD mouse model after intranasal administration of the secretome obtained from MSCs exposed to AD mouse brain homogenates under *in vitro* conditions. As a result, MSCs transplantation in AD, results in improved memory, accelerated amyloid plaque clearance, decreased neuronal inflammation, and stimulation of endogenous neurogenesis, all of which can be imitated by using the MSCs derived secretome, indicating that the paracrine effects of MSCs play an important role (**Fig. 12.1**).

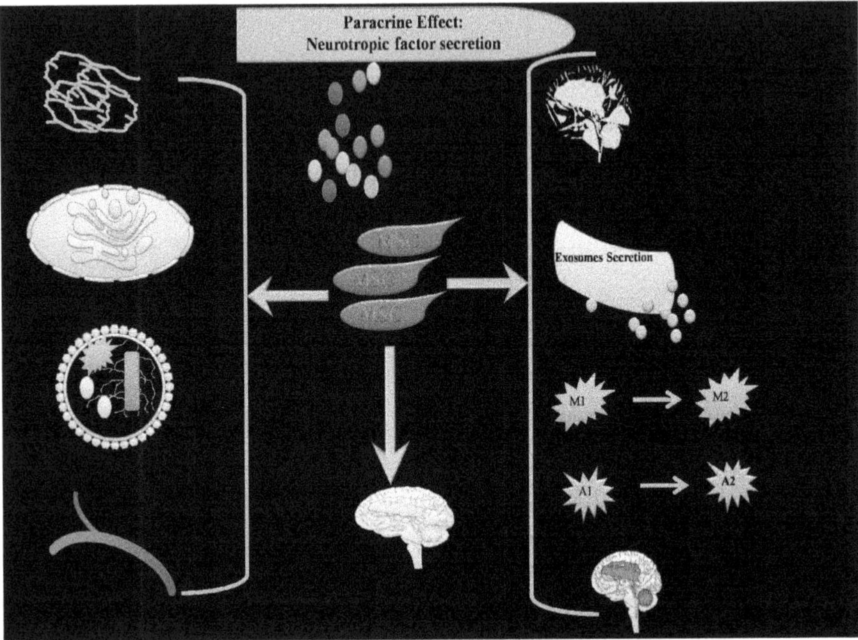

Figure 12.1: Mechanism proposed for MSC therapy in the treatment of Alzheimer's disease: Cell replacement, paracrine effects, exosome secretion, immune modulation, angiogenesis stimulation, endogenous neurogenesis stimulation, increased Aβ and NFTs clearance, improved autophagy, and BBB(blood brain barrier), NVU (neural-vascular unit) renormalization are all thought to be mechanisms by which MSCs exert their effects. The figure was created using Motifolio tool kit (WWW.Motifolio.com).

Another important mechanism for the therapeutic use of MSCs is neuro-inflammation modulation, as neuro-inflammation plays an important role in the pathogenesis of AD. Several studies have shown that mesenchymal stem cells have the ability to convert pro-inflammatory phenotypes M1 and A1 of microglia and astrocytes to anti-inflammatory phenotypes M2 and A2, thereby relieving the neuro-inflammatory response and neuronal damage in AD (Wei et al., 2018; Zhao et al., 2018; Qin et al., 2021). Zhao et al., (2018) revealed that intracerebral transplanting of menstrual blood derived MSCs increased the memory and spatial learning of amyloid precursor protein/ presenilin 1 mice (APP/PS1 mice). Furthermore, the expression of pro-inflammatory cytokines was significantly reduced, indicating that the positive impacts were caused by the microglia switching from a pro-inflammatory to an anti-inflammatory phenotype. When Wharton's jelly derived MSCs (WJ-MSCs) were transplanted intravenously, they improved memory and spatial learning in APP/PS1 mice, while decreasing Aβ deposition and soluble Aβ levels (Xie et al., 2016). WJ-MSCs were found to significantly reduce the pro-inflammatory cytokines IL-1β and TNFα, while increasing the expression of the anti-inflammatory cytokine IL-10. Adipose-derived MSCs (AD-MSCs) transplanted intracerebrally were found to reduce -amyloid (Aβ) peptide deposition and restore memory/learning functioning in APP/S1 transgenic mice (Ma et al.., 2013). MSCs derived from the umbilical cord secrete sICAM-1 (soluble intracellular adhesion molecules-1) which induces the expression of neprilysin (an Aβ-degrading enzyme) and thus facilitates Aβ clearance. MSCs also reduce the burden *via* internalization and Aβ degradation of the endosomal-lysosomal pathway (Naaldiik et al., 2017; Zhao et al., 2018; Santamaria et al., 2021).

Mitochondrial transfer is also thought to be a promising and new mechanism of stem cell therapy for tissue damage. Several studies have demonstrated the potential use of MSCs in transferring healthy mitochondria to dying neurons in order to restore energy metabolism and prevent neuron death (Hayakawa et al., 2016). For mitochondrial transfer, various methods such as tunneling nanotube (TNT), cell fusion, and extracellular vesicle (EV) can be used. Various brain ischemia models have shown that mitochondrial transfer plays a role in AD as well. Zhang et al. (2020) reported that hUC-MSCs can donate healthy mitochondria to okadaic acid (OA) treated SH-SY5Y cells, resulting in mitochondrial function restoration in an Alzheimer's disease cell model. Extracellular vesicle (EV), TNT (tunneling nanotube), or cell fusion can all be used to transfer mitochondria (Gomzikova et al., 2021). Other mechanisms implicated for MSC therapy in AD pathogenesis include increased autophagy, decreased ROS, and renormalization of BBB and NVU (neural-vascular unit) (Guo et al., 2021).

Conclusion

The strong, statistically significant and biologically relevant result of mesenchymal stem cell (MSCs) therapy, has opened new horizons of research and gave a hope for curing of diseases, which till date are uncurable-like Alzheimer's disease. Promising results have been obtained during preclinical trials of MSC therapy. MSC have been found to give relieve from AD pathology by different approaches such enhancing anti-inflammatory cytokines, reducing levels of pro-inflammatory cytokines, synaptogenesis, neuronal regeneration, secreting angiogenic and neurotrophic factors, and mitochondrial transfer. Such evidence based results make the mesenchymal stem cells (MSCs) strong candidates, for being fully explored and researched, in order to make them a readily available therapeutic agents against different ailments.

Future Perspective:

As of now mesenchymal stem cells (MSCs) have shown promising results both *in-vitro* and *in-vivo* (Animal model) studies in comparison to that of conventional therapies used against Alzheimer's disease (AD). There are reports that show success rate is not same in human clinical trials. As such there is:

- One need to develop such AD models which would be much more similar to human AD that would be helpful in efficient transition from basic research to clinical trials.
- Understand molecular cross talks of MSCs, during their therapeutic intervention.
- Engineering of MSCs, so as to ensure their specific therapeutic effect.

References:

1. Alipour M, et al. (2019). Stem cell therapy in Alzheimer's disease: possible benefits and limiting drawbacks. Mol Biol Reports 46(1): 1425–1446.
2. Choi SS, et al. (2014). Alzheimer's disease and stem cell therapy. Exp Neurobiol 23(1): 45.
3. Cong L. (2022). The Role of Mesenchymal Stem Cells in Regulating Astrocytes-Related Synapse Dysfunction in Early Alzheimer 's disease. Front Neurosci 16: 927256
4. Cooney D, et al. (2016). Mesenchymal stem cells enhance nerve regeneration in a rat sciatic nerve repair and hindlimb transplant model. Scientific Reports 6(1).
5. Cummings J, et al. (2020). Alzheimer's disease drug development pipeline: 2020. Alzheimers Dement (NY) 6: e12050.

6. Dominici ML, et al. (2006). Minimal criteria for defining multipotent mesenchymal stromal cells. The International Society for Cellular Therapy position statement. Cytotherapy 8(4): 315-317.
7. Doruk H, et al. (2010). The relationship between body mass index and incidental mild cognitive impairment, Alzheimer's disease and vascular dementia in elderly. J Nut Health Aging14: 834-838.
8. Duncan T, & Valenzuela M. (2017). Alzheimer's disease, dementia, and stem cell therapy. Stem Cell Res Therapy 8(1): 1-9.
9. Ferri CP, et al. (2005). Alzheimer's Disease International. Global prevalence of dementia: a Delphi consensus study. Lancet 366:2112-2117.
10. Fevrier B, et al. (2014). Cells release prions in association with exosomes. Proc Natl Acad Sci USA. 101(26): 9683–8.
11. Friedenstein AJ, et al. (1974). Stromal cells responsible for transferring the microenvironment of the hemopoietic tissues: cloning in vitro and retransplantation in vivo. Transplant 17(4): 331-340.
12. Gugjoo MB. (2022). Mesenchymal Stem Cells Therapeutic Applications in Central Nervous System Disorders. In: Therapeutic Applications of Mesenchymal Stem Cells in Veterinary Medicine. Springer Nature. pp. 163-212.
13. Guo M, et al. (2020). Mesenchymal stem cell-derived exosome: A promising alternative in the therapy of Alzheimer's disease. Alzheimer's Res Therapy 12(1): 1-14.
14. Hayakawa K, et al. (2016). Transfer of mitochondria from astrocytes to neurons after stroke. Nature 535(7613): 551-555.
15. Hernández AE, & García E. (2021). Mesenchymal stem cell therapy for Alzheimer's disease. Stem Cells Int 2021: 7834421.
16. Herrup K. (2010). Reimagining Alzheimer's disease – an age-based hypothesis. J Neurosci 30: 16755-16762.
17. Imhof A, et al. (2007). Morphological substrates of cognitive decline in nonagenarians and centenarians: A new paradigm? J Neurol Sci 257: 72-79.
18. Kim J, et al. (2020). Mesenchymal stem cell therapy and Alzheimer's disease: current status and future perspectives.J Alzheimer's Dis 77(1): 1–14.
19. Kim, J., Lee, Y., Lee, S., Kim, K., Song, M., & Lee, J. (2020). Mesenchymal stem cell therapy and Alzheimer's disease: current status and future perspectives. *Journal of Alzheimer's Disease, 77*(1), 1-14.

20. Knopman DS. (2001). An overview of common non-Alzheimer dementias. Clin Ger Med17: 281.
21. Kolios G, & Moodley Y. (2013). Introduction to stem cells and regenerative medicine. Respiration85(1): 3–10.
22. Liu H, et al. (2021). Molecular mechanisms of altered adult hippocampal neurogenesis in Alzheimer's disease. Mechan Ageing Dev 195: 111452.
23. Liu X, et al. (2020). Stem cell therapy for Alzheimer's disease. World J Stem Cells, 12(8): 787– 802.
24. Ma T, et al. (2013). Intracerebral transplantation of adipose-derived mesenchymal stem cells alternatively activates microglia and ameliorates neuropathological deficits in Alzheimer's disease mice. Cell Transplant 22(1_suppl): 113-126.
25. Mann DMA, et al. (1987). Topographic distribution of senile plaques, neurofibrillary tangles in the brains of non demented persons of different age. Neuropath App Neurobiol 13:123-139.
26. Masako N, et al. (2020). Bone marrow-derived mesenchymal stem cells improve cognitive impairment in an Alzheimer's disease model by increasing the expression of microRNA-146a in hippocampus. Scientific Reports10: 10772.
27. Meek PD, et al. (1998). Economic considerations in Alzheimer's Disease. Pharmacother18: 68–73.
28. Mengtian G, et al. (2020).Mesenchymal stem cell-derived exosome: a promising alternative in the therapy of Alzheimer's disease. Alzheimer's Res Therapy12: 109.
29. Park BN, et al. (2018). In vivo tracking of intravenously injected mesenchymal stem cells in an Alzheimer's animal model. Cell Transplant 27(8): 1203-1209.
30. Park BN, et al. (2020). Therapeutic effect of mesenchymal stem cells in an animal model of Alzheimer's disease evaluated by β-amyloid positron emission tomography imaging. Australian New Zealand J Psychiatry 54(9): 883-891.
31. Qin C, et al. (2021). Functional Mechanism of Bone Marrow-Derived Mesenchymal Stem Cells in the Treatment of Animal Models with Alzheimer's Disease: Inhibition of Neuroinflammation. J Inflamm Res 14: 4761.
32. Reisberg B. (1983). Alzheimer's disease. The Standard Reference. Macmillan, London and New York.

33. Rossor M, Mountjoy CQ. (1986). Post-mortem neurochemical changes in Alzheimer's disease compared with normal ageing. Can J Neurol Sci 13:499-502.
34. Santamaria G, et al. (2021). Intranasal delivery of mesenchymal stem cell secretome repairs the brain of Alzheimer's mice. Cell Death & Different 28(1): 203-218.
35. Shen Y, et al. (2018). Cognitive decline, dementia. Alzheimers Dis Presbycusis 12: 394.
36. Sivandzade F, & Cucullo L. (2021). Regenerative stem cell therapy for neurodegenerative diseases: An overview. Int J Mol Sci 22(4): 2153.
37. Staff NP, et al. (2019). Mesenchymal stromal cell therapies for neurodegenerative diseases. Mayo Clinic Proc 94(5): 892–905.
38. van der Kant R, et al. (2020). Amyloid-β-independent regulators of tau pathology in Alzheimer disease. Nature Rev Neurosci 21(1): 21-35.
39. Wei L, et al. (2017). Stem cell transplantation therapy for multifaceted therapeutic benefits after stroke. Progress Neurobiol 157: 49-78.
40. Wei Y, et al. (2018). Anti-inflammatory effects of bone marrow mesenchymal stem cells on mice with Alzheimer's disease. Exp Therap Med 16(6): 5015-5020.
41. Xie ZH, et al. (2016). Wharton's Jelly-derived mesenchymal stem cells alleviate memory deficits and reduce amyloid-β deposition in an APP/PS1 transgenic mouse model. Clin Exp Med 16(1): 89-98.
42. Zhang Z, et al. (2020). Mesenchymal stem cell-conditioned medium improves mitochondrial dysfunction and suppresses apoptosis in okadaic acid-treated SH-SY5Y cells by extracellular vesicle mitochondrial transfer. J Alzheimer's Dis 78(3): 1161-1176.
43. Zhao Y, et al. (2018). Transplantation of human menstrual blood-derived mesenchymal stem cells alleviates Alzheimer's disease-like pathology in APP/PS1 transgenic mice. Front Mol Neurosci 11: 140.

CHAPTER THIRTEEN

Mesenchymal Stem Cells for Diabetes

Faliq Iqbal Bhat and **Asia Mushtaq Zargar**
Department of Biochemistry, University of Kashmir, Hazratbal, Srinagar, J&K, India

Abstract

Diabetes mellitus (DM) is a chronic condition that can lead to a number of systemic compication. The potential treatments for DM-related problems include stem cell-based therapy which has gain a wide attention.Due to their immunosuppressive traits, anti-inflammatory qualities, and differentiation potential, Mesenchymal stem cell (MSC) based therapies are frequently regarded as the best stem cell-based treatment for managing diabetes. In the treatment of diabetic cardiomyopathy, diabetic polyneuropathy, diabetic nephropathy, diabetic retinopathy, and diabetic wounds, MSCs are effective therapeutic agents. Type 1 diabetes is a chronic disorder characterized by the destruction of pancreatic Islet beta -cells. Through paracrine actions such angiogenic, cytoprotective, anti-inflammatory, mitogenic, and anti-apoptotic properties, MSCs transplantation into diabetic rats may prevent apoptosis of injured pancreatic beta cells and increase regeneration of endogenous progenitor cells. A high-fat diet (HFD) and streptozotocin (STZ)-induced T2DM rat model can be reversed by intravenous administration of bone marrow-derived MSCs by enhancing insulin secretion, activating the insulin-signaling pathway, and increasing the expression and membrane transposition of glucose transporters (GLUT).

Key words: Diabetes mellitus, mesenchymal stem cells, apoptosis, insulin signaling,

Introduction

Diabetes mellitus has emerged as a foremost health care problem globally. According to International Diabetes Federation, currently there are 371 million people alive with diabetes mellitus worldwide and this number is anticipated to increase to 552 million by 2030 i.e. a 51% raise. The prevalence of Diabetes Mellitus is increasing at an alarming rate worldwide with 90% having Type 2 Diabetes Mellitus (T2DM). Diabetes is considered so dangerous because of its ability to affect almost all vital organs like kidneys, eyes and heart. Consumption of high calorie diet and sedentary lifestyle disorders is rapidly becoming the most important health issue in most of the developed countries.

Potential pathogenic mechanisms in diabetes include hyper glycemia, Insulin resistance, oxidative stress, and inflammation that could culminate in the increased susceptibility to complications. Genetic background and consequently genetic factors might have role in both onset and progression of T2DM related complications. Diabetic person unfortunately suffers from additional pathologies which are retinopathy, cardiomyopathy, nephropathy and neuropathy. Hyper glycaemic state can lead to formation of pathological microenvironment that alter normal cellular process or cellular changes. Cellular changes in diabetes is well known established and a little is known in regards to how diabetes alter the function of Mesenchymal stem cells (MSC) (van de Vyver, 2017). Mesenchymal stem cell which is a multipotent mesenchymal stromal cell, is self-renewing and can be found in all postnatal organs and tissues. MSC have main functional characteristics which are immunomodulatory ability, capability of self-renewal, and differentiation into tissues of mesodermal origin such as chondroblasts, osteoblasts or adipocytes with variable expression of several molecules likeCD105, CD73, CD19, CD166, CD54 and CD49 and lack expression of surface marker CD14, CD45. Transcription factors such as octamer-binding transcription factor 4 (OCT-4) and homeobox protein NANOG are also expressed by MSC (Pittenger et al., 1999; Sabapathy et al., 2012). MSC are able to differentiate into different cell types like cardiomyocytes, vascular endothelial cells, neurons, hepatocytes, epithelial cells and adipocytes. Differentiation into different cell types make them potentially important for treatment of debilitating human diseases. Such capacity of multipotent differentiation with characteristics of self-renewal and ability to modulate immune response make MSCs potential therapeutic candidate for treatment of diabetic mellitus and its complications.

Type 1 diabetes which is a chronic disorder, an insulin dependent auto immune disorder characterized by selective and irreversible destruction of insulin producing beta cells within pancreatic islets of Langerhans. Insulin replacement is the current main therapeutic approach and nowadays transplantation of pancreatic islets is successfully applied to treat diabetes. Studies have shown that MSC transplantation improves metabolic profiles of diabetic animal models. Transplanted MSCs show trans-differentiation into insulin producing cells (IPC) that show therapeutic action (Gugjoo, 2022). It has been revealed in reports that MSCs, under hypoxia environment and *in vitro* gene manipulation, produce several cytokines such as IGF-1, VEGF and HGF, capable of promoting survival of surrounding cells through paracrine mechanism. The influence of bioactive secretion by MSC mediates functional outcome. MSCs regenerative properties for diabetes are vascular development, anti-inflammation and anti-fibrosis (**Fig. 13.1**).

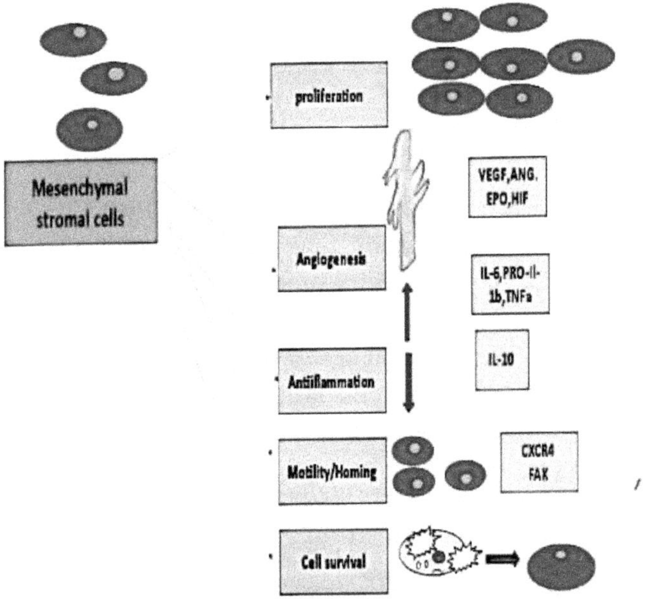

Figure 13.1: Therapeutic effects of mesenchymal stem cells, ANG-angiopoietin; EPO-Erythropoietin; FAK-focal adhesion kinase; HIF-hypoxia inducible factor's- tumour necrosis factor; VEGF-vascular endothelial growth factor.

Since MSC shows ability to produce trophic effect on stem cells, it can be summarized that transplanted MSCs may play crucial role in hyperglycaemia reversal in diabetic animal models. Regenerative medicine is rapidly evolving, which is paving way for normal therapeutic interventions like tissue engineering and cellular therapies, thus reshaping the biomedical field. Different cell subsets obtained from human embryonic and adult tissues from disparate sources (including bone marrow, umbilical cord, amniotic fluid, placenta, adipose tissue shows remarkable plasticity and have sparked research endeavours for using these cells for numerous condition including diabetes and its complications. MSCs have been used to generate insulin producing cells, enhance islet engraftment and survival and to treat diabetic ulcers and limb ischemia in context of diabetic research (Karnieli et al. 2007). It has been seen that MSC inoculum improved metabolic control in experimental models of type 2 diabetes. Trials in T2DM patients and rat models through non randomized way shows positive impact of bone arrow derived mononuclear cells on metabolism i.e reduction of insulin resistance, improvement in insulin secretion, activation the insulin signalling system, and increase in the expression and membrane transposition of glucose transporters (GLUT).

To study the effects of autologous MSCs inoculum in rat models of T2DM (Induced by HF- diet for 2 weeks followed by suboptimal dose of beta cell toxin streptozotocin (STZ) to induce hyperglycaemic state). The autologous MSCs were administered either (1 or 3) weeks after STZ treatment. An enhanced insulin secretion along with improved metabolic control were measured and increased islet number were measured in animals receiving MSC particularly when MSC were given in early (7 days) after STZ treatment. A novel data that emerge from this study indicates that MSCs therapies may be associated with improved insulin sensitivity. This may occur through signalling insulin response substrate (IRS-1), AKT phosphorylation and GLUT- 4 translocation on cell membrane upon insulin administration in liver muscle, adipose tissue of animals which received inoculum (Shibata et al., 2008). Thus, MSC offer new opportunities in treatment of diabetes, but also questions particularly related to safety and efficacy that need to be addressed (Karnieli et al., 2007; Ding et al., 2009; Fiorina et al., 2009; Madec et al., 2009; Berman et al., 2010; Lu et al., 2011). Researchers have shown the tremendous therapeutic capabilities of MSC e.g., use of autologous MSC for diabetic neuropathy, nephropathy, cardiomyopathy and wound healing.

MSCs in diabetic cardiomyopathy

Diabetic mellitus patients suffering from ventricular dysfunctions in absence of either coronary heart disease, valvular heart disease or hypertension is defined as Diabetic cardiomyopathy (DCM). Chronic hyperglycaemia is responsible for myocardial remodelling that results in progression of DCM, characterized by hypertrophy and apoptosis of extracellular matrix (ECM), resulting in collagen deposition. Progression of DCM is due to decreased activity of MMP-2, increased collagen accumulation, increased activity of pro apoptotic factor MMP-9 (responsible for apoptosis of endothelial cells and reduction in capillary density) (Camp et al., 2003) (**Fig 13. 2**).

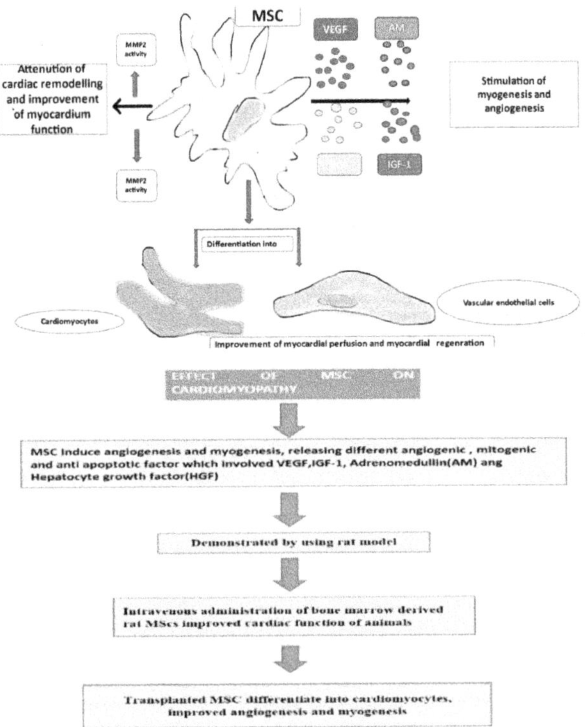

Fig. 13.2: Effects of transplanted MSCs on diabetic cardiomyopathy. (a) MSCs increase the activity of MMP-2 and decrease the activity of MMP-9 and attenuate cardiac remodelling. (b) MSCs produce VEGF, IGF-1, AM, HGF and stimulate myogenesis and angiogenesis in damaged myocardium. (c) Through differentiation into cardiomyocytes and vascular endothelial

cells, MSCs improve myocardial perfusion and myocardium regeneration. Abbreviations: AM, adrenomedullin; HGF, hepatocyte growth factor; IGF-1, insulin-like growth factor-1; MMP, matrix metalloproteinase; MSC, mesenchymal stem cell; VEGF, vascular endothelial growth factor.

MSCs treatment for Polyneuropathy

Common complication of diabetic mellitus is polyneuropathy (a damage to nerve fibres). There is neural cell degeneration and decreased blood flow. Angiogenic cytokines like FGF and EGF could be useful for treatment of diabetic polyneuropathy (Yoon et al., 2005; Kinnaird et al., 2004; Wang et al., 2009). MSC in diabetic rats are able to secrete FGF and VEGF and could be effective and new therapeutic agent for treatment of diabetic poly neuropathy (Kinnaird et al., 2004; Wang et al., 2009). Although MSCs can differentiate into brain cells such astrocytes, oligodendrocytes, and Schwann cells, this was not observed in diabetic rats after MSC implantation (Shibata et al. 2008). However, transplanted MSCs improved the blood-retinal barrier, alleviating diabetic retinopathy in STZ diabetic mice by releasing paracrine factors and differentiating into photoreceptor and glial-like cells in the retina (Wange et al., 2010) (**Fig. 13.3**).

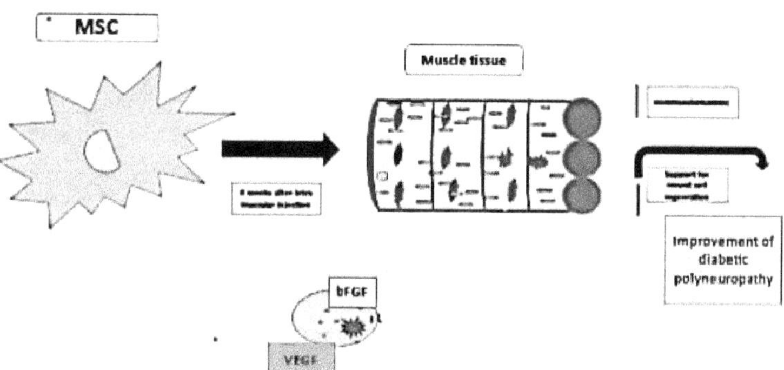

Fig.13.3: Effects of MSCs treatment on diabetic polyneuropathy. Four weeks after intramuscular injection, MSCs settled in the gap between muscle fibres, through production of bFGF and VEGF, induces neovascularization and support regeneration of neural cells that results with improvement of diabetic polyneuropathy. Abbreviations: bFGF, basic fibroblast growth factor; MSC, mesenchymal stem cell; VEGF, vascular endothelial growth factor

Diabetes related nephropathy

Diabetes-related nephropathy, a progressive kidney disease caused by angiopathy of the capillaries supplying the kidney glomeruli, can be prevented and treated by administering MSCs (Ezquer et al., 2008). Murine MSCs injected into mice model of renal injury show that these cells develop into renal cells, engraft in injured kidneys, and control the immune response, effectively treating diabetic nephropathy (Lee et al., 2006; Ezquer et al., 2008). As MSCs are able to reconstruct necrotic portions of diabetic kidneys, systemic treatment of MSCs to diabetic mice improve kidney function and regenerate glomerular shape (Lee et al., 2006; Ezquer et al., 2008). The ability of MSCs to develop into insulin-producing beta cells followed by a decrease in glycemia and glycosuria can prevent renal cells further damage and thus MSC can prevent diabetic nephropathy (Ezquer et al., 2008).

MSCs treatment for Diabetic wounds

In Diabetic mellitus patients prolonged wound healing due to reduced production of growth factors, impaired angiogenesis and compromised collagen matrix synthesis occur. Additionally there is disturbance in production and functionality of growth factor such as transforming factor (TGF- BETA, Epidermal growth factor (EGF), Vascular endothelial growth factor (VEGF), Platelet derived growth factor (PDGF) and Keratinocyte growth factor (KGF) in diabetes (Spanheimer et al., 1992; Shibata et al., 2008). MSCs improve wound healing in diabetic wounds of rat and mice. MSCs injection result in moderate KGF and significant increase in factors like TGF, EGF, VEGF and PDGF that are responsible for repair of injured tissues and is crucial and important for wound healing. Efficacy of MSCs is also shown in case of ulceration in diabetic patients. For closing and healing diabetic foot ulceration autologous biograft composed of skin fibroblast seeded on biodegradable collagen membrane with autologous BM-MSCs. Difference are seen in the efficacy between systemic and local MSC therapy for wound healing and better effects are noticed after local administration of MSCs due to presence of arterial venous shunt in diabetic skin which complicate migration of systemically injected MSCs towards wound (Le Blanc et al., 2005; Wu et al., 2007).

Conclusion

It can be concluded that MSC having self-renewal, immunomodulatory and differential capacity are expected to become promising therapeutic agent for improvement of cardiac function and treatment of cardiomyopathy, neuropathy, nephropathy and wound healing in diabetic patients. MSCs can be defined as novel and efficient therapeutic agent in treatment of complication of diabetes. Through paracrine actions in the form of growth factors or cytokines, MSCs may have a significant impact on pancreatic repair and functional improvement. MSCs may prevent apoptosis of damaged pancreatic cells and promoting regeneration of endogenous progenitor cells which may help in increasing the mass of functioning pancreatic β-cells. MSCs have been employed to treat diabetic ulcers, to produce insulin-producing cells in order to fight autoimmunity, improve islet engraftment and survival. MSC have a great capacity for proliferation and renewal, which is necessary for maintaining long-lasting therapeutic effects suitable for clinical use.

References

1. Berman DM, et al. (2010). Mesenchymal stem cells enhance allogeneic islet engraftment in nonhuman primates. Diabetes 59: 2558–2568.
2. Camp TM, et al. (2003). Gelatinase B (MMP-9) an apoptotic factor in diabetic transgenic mice. Diabetologia 46: 1438–1445.
3. Ding Y, et al. (2009). Mesenchymal stem cells prevent the rejection of fully allogenic islet grafts by the immune suppressive activity of matrix metalloproteinase-2 and -9. Diabetes 58:1797–1806.
4. Ezquer FE, et al. (2008). Systemic administration of multipotent mesenchymal stromal cells reverts hyperglycemia and prevents nephropathy in type 1 diabetic mice. Biol Blood Marrow Transplant 14: 631–640.
5. Fiorina P, et al. (2009). Immunomodulatory function of bone marrow-derived mesenchymal stem cells in experimental autoimmune type 1 diabetes. J Immunol 183: 993–1004.
6. Gugjoo MB. (2022). Mesenchymal Stem Cells Therapeutic Applications in Endocrine Disorders. In: Therapeutic Applications of Mesenchymal Stem Cells in Veterinary Medicine. Springer Nature. pp. 375-390
7. Karnieli O, et al. (2007). Generation of insulin-producing cells from human bone marrow mesenchymal stem cells by genetic manipulation. Stem Cells 25: 2837–2844.
8. Kinnaird T, et al. (2004). Local delivery of marrow derived stromal cells augments collateral perfusion through paracrine mechanisms. Circulation 109: 1543–1549.

9. Le Blanc K, & Pittenger M. (2005). Mesenchymal stem cells: Progress toward promise. Cytotherapy 7:36–45.
10. Lee RH, et al. (2006). Multipotent stromal cells from humanmarrow home to and promote repair of pancreatic islets and renal glomeruli in diabetic NOD/scid mice. Proc Natl Acad Sci USA 103: 17438–17443.
11. Lee RH, et al. (2006). Multipotent stromal cells from human marrow home to and promote repair of pancreatic islets and renal glomeruli in diabetic NOD/scid mice. Proc Natl Acad Sci USA 103: 17438–17443.
12. Lu D, et al. (2011). Comparison of bone marrow mesenchymal stem cells with bone marrow-derived mononuclear cells for treatment of diabetic critical limb ischemia and foot ulcer: a double-blind, randomized, controlled trial. Diabetes Res Clin Pract 92: 26–36.
13. Madec AM, et al. Mesenchymal stem cells protect NOD mice from diabetes by inducing regulatory T cells. Diabetologia 52:1391–1399.
14. Medina A, et al. (2005). Pathophysiology of chronic nonhealing wounds. J Burn Care Rehabil 26: 306–319.
15. Pittenger MF, et al. (1999). Multilineage potential of adult human mesenchymal stem cells. Science 284:143– 147.
16. Sabapathy V, et al. (2012). Long-term cultured human term placenta-derived mesenchymal stem cells of maternal origin displays plasticity. Stem Cells Int2012: 174328.
17. Shibata T, et al. (2008). Transplantation of bone mar row-derived mesenchymal stem cells improves diabetic polyneuro pathy in rats. Diabetes 57: 3099–31071937.
18. Shibata T, et al. (2008). Transplantation of bone marrow-derived mesenchymal stem cells improves diabetic polyneuropathy in rats. Diabetes 57: 3099–3107.
19. Spanheimer RG. (1992). Correlation between decreased collagen production in diabetic animals and in cells exposed to diabetic serum: Response to insulin. Matrix 12: 101–107.
20. van de Vyver M. (2017). Intrinsic mesenchymal stem cell dysfunction in diabetes mellitus: implications for autologous cell therapy. Stem Cells Dev 26(14):1042–1053.
21. Wang X, et al. (2009). Hsp20-engineered mesenchymal stem cells are resistant to oxidative stress via enhanced activation of Akt and increased secretion of growth factors. Stem Cells 27: 3021–3031.

22. Wu Y, et al. (2007). Mesenchymal stem cells enhance wound healing through differentiation and angiogenesis. Stem Cells 25: 2648–2659.9.
23. Yang Z, et al. (2010). Amelioration of diabetic retinopathy by engrafted human adipose-derived mesenchymal stem cells in streptozotocin diabetic rats. Graefes Arch Clin Exp Ophthalmol 248: 1415–1422.
24. Yoon YS, et al. (2005). Progressive attenuation of myocardial vascular endothelial growth factor expression is a seminal event in diabetic cardiomyopathy: Restoration of microvascular homeostasis and recovery of cardiac function in diabetic cardiomyopathy. Circulation 111(16): 2073-85.

CHAPTER FOURTEEN

Mesenchymal Stem Cells for Multiple Sclerosis

Toyeeba Hassan

[1]*Centre of Research for Development (CORD), University of Kashmir, Hazratbal, Srinagar, J&K*

Abstract

Multiple sclerosis is an inflammatory illness of the central nervous system that causes demyelination and neurodegeneration while also abnormally activating the immune system. Mesenchymal stem cells have immunomodulatory and immunosuppressive capabilities, according to studies on experimental multiple sclerosis models utilising mesenchymal stem cells in clinical trials. The central nervous system is affected by the chronic autoimmune inflammatory illness known as multiple sclerosis (MS) (CNS). Autologous and allogenic transplantation of mesenchymal stem cells (MSCs) has been established as a successful therapeutic approach in MS in an effort to find a suitable treatment for reducing neurological symptoms and remyelination. MSCs are a diverse subset of non-hematopoietic, pluripotent stromal cells that can be extracted from bone marrow, adipose tissue, placenta, and other sources. Due to their capacity for differentiation, migration, immune-modulation, and neurodegeneration, MSCs have significant therapeutic effects. Animal models of MS, such as experimental autoimmune encephalomyelitis, have been used to test MSCs. Researchers have also evaluated genetically altered MSCs, MSC-derived conditioned media, or a combination of these. In this chapter, we highlight the experimental animal model studies that have been used MSCs as a potential MS treatment.

Keywords: Mesenchymal stem cells; Multiple sclerosis; Immunomodulation; Immunosuppression; Pluripotent stromal cells

Introduction

Multiple sclerosis (MS) is an autoimmune, neurodegenerative, and chronic inflammatory illness that affects the central nervous system (CNS) (Confavreux and Vukusic, 2006; Bosca et al., 2008; Racosta and Kimpinski, 2016). MS is among the most prevalent neurological conditions that impair young individuals, and the incidence of the disease is two times higher in women than in men (Walczak et al., 2013; Zafranskaya et al., 2013; Li et al., 2014). Motor and sensory impairment are caused by the destruction of myelin sheaths, which is accompanied by inflammation, demyelination, and axonal loss (Harris et al., 2018). The operational loss of oligodendrocytes, the influx of leukocytes into the central nervous system (CNS), and astrogliosis are the typical characteristics of these injured areas (Connick et al., 2012; Dahbour et al., 2017). Relapsing-remitting MS (RRMS), which is defined by acute neurological inflammation followed by practically full remission between attacks, typically starts with an acute relapse episode (Harris et al., 2018). The majority of MS patients, however, advance to the chronic secondary progressive MS (SPMS) phase, which is marked by neurodegeneration and motor and cognitive impairment (Bosca et al., 2008; Riordan et al., 2018). Progressive neurological MS and primary relapsing MS are two other kinds of MS. Despite the availability of numerous pharmaceutical treatments, such as monoclonal antibodies and oral immunosuppressants, which may have major adverse effects, such as raising the patient's risk of infections and cancer, MS is still incurable (Orack et al., 2015; Walczak et al., 2013). The need for regeneration therapy is highlighted by the fact that while these treatments reduce symptoms and relapse rates, they have no clinical benefit once the patient enters the neurodegenerative SPMS phase of the disease (Dahbour et al., 2017). Current research is concentrating on the therapeutic effects of stem cells for the treatment of numerous autoimmune and degenerative disorders, including MS, notably SPMS, based on their anti-inflammatory, immunosuppressive, and neuroregenerative properties (Connick et al., 2012; De Paula et al., 2015; Atkins and Freedman, 2017). Additionally, it is now widely acknowledged that stem cells effectively treat autoimmune disorders including graft-versus-host disease and systemic lupus as well as neurological diseases like amyotrophic lateral sclerosis (Lunn et al., 2014; Alchi et al., 2013). Mesenchymal stem cells (MSCs), a type of stem cell that can be conveniently separated from bone marrow, adipose tissue, and many other sources, have several properties that make them the top choice for cell therapy (Freedman et al., 2010; Bai et al., 2012). These include their low immunogenic potential, ease of expansion in vitro, lack of ethical issues, ease of isolation, amenability to autologous injection safety, and low tumorigenic potential as well as their capacity to transdifferentiate into multipotent cells (Meamar et al., 2016; Cohen et al., 2018; Genc et al., 2019).

Sources of MSCs

There are numerous sources of MSCs that have been used in experimental MS, but the majority of research have used bone marrow-derived MSCs (BM-MSCs) from humans, mice usually female C57BL/6 mice Wistar rats and male Lewis rats. MSCs can also be taken from healthy or ill people or animals, as was the case in research using human BM-MSCs (hBM-MSCs) from patients who had spinal cord injuries or MSCs taken from mice that had EAE (Lotfy et al., 2020).Adipose-derived stem cells (AD-MSCs), which are also taken from humans and occasionally from thin and obese people as well as mice, notably male BALB/c mice, are another source of MSCs (Strong et al., 2016; Yousefi et al., 2016). Other sources include rat placental stem cells, mouse bone-chip MSCs, human umbilical cord MSCs, and human periodontal ligament stem cells (hPDL-SCs) (Human embryonic stem cells (hESCs) and Wharton's jelly (WJ-MSCs) (**Fig. 14.1**) (Lotfy et al., 2020).

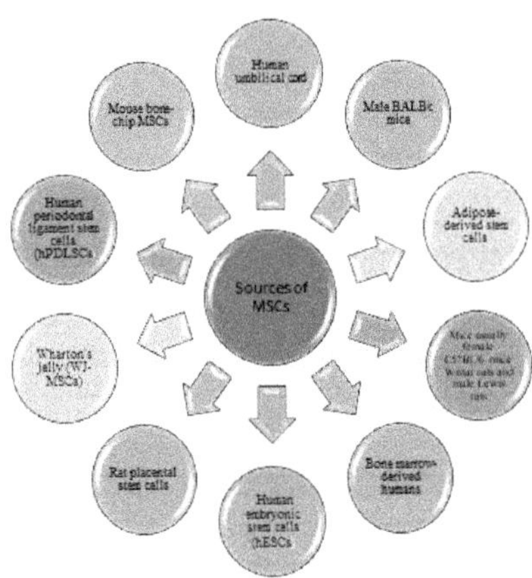

Fig. 14.1: MSCs from different sources evaluated for multiple sclerosis

MSCs role in treating MS and Experimental Autoimmune Encephalopathy

Immune tolerance and T cell energy may be brought on by systemic administration of murine MSCs to Experimental Autoimmune Encephalopathy (EAE) animal models, according to research (Zappia et al., 2005). Additionally, after being given systemically to EAE animals, green fluorescent protein (GFP)-labeled MSCs moved into CNS lesions and lymph nodes and reduced illness symptoms (Zappia et al., 2005; Gerdoni et al., 2007). In an EAE model, human-derived MSCs have been shown by Gordon and colleagues to have significant ameliorative benefits with only minimal CNS invasion (Gordon, et al., 2008). Another group has also proven the penetration of MSCs into the CNS and their ameliorative effects on an animal model of EAE (Schafer et al., 2008). It has been proposed that MSCs from rodents and humans can combine to form heterokaryon in the cerebellum of mice (Kemp et al., 2011). Another study found that allogeneic MSCs could lessen EAE. They stated that the lowering of neuroinflammatory cytokines including IFN-c and IL-17 was related to this ameliorative impact. It's interesting to note that they discovered that in vivo immunological rejection and total loss of the suppressive activity of MSCs after prestimulation with IFN-c (Rafei et al., 2009). Other researchers have demonstrated that intravenously injected human MSCs accumulate in myelin damaged areas of EAE mice and reduce demyelination (Gordon, et al., 2008). However, Grigoriadis and colleagues showed that whereas intracerebroventricular delivery of autologous MSCs to mice with moderate EAE was linked to a beneficial effect, it was unable to lessen severe EAE and was linked to certain negative consequences (Grigoriadis et al., 2011). Human placental MSCs were intracranially injected into EAE mice, and this reduced the severity of the condition and improved animal's survival (Fisher-Shoval et al., 2012). Additionally, intrathecal administration of brain progenitors generated from MSCs to EAE mice demonstrated notable ameliorative and neuroprotective effects. These cells are a variant of bone marrow MSCs with immunomodulatory, neural progenitor, and a diminished capacity for mesoderm development (Harris et al., 2012). Examination of these progenitor cells in MS patients revealed that they had immunomodulatory functions and phenotypes that are similar to those of progenitor cells from healthy individuals (Harris and Faroqui, 2012). MSCs produced from human umbilical cords have also reduced inflammation in EAE mice (Liu et al., 2012). Adipose-derived MSCs were infused into EAE animals to reduce neuroinflammation and to keep glycogen synthase kinase 3b (GSK3b) in an inactive state (Tafreshi et al., 2014). Yousefi and colleagues recently compared the effectiveness of adipose-tissue MSC injection routes via intraperitoneal and intravenous routes in EAE mice. They found that intraperitoneal infusion, as opposed to intravenous injection, had a greater impact on raising splenic Treg counts and IL-4 levels, and lowering IFN-c and cell infiltration in the brain. However, both injection methods similarly reduced IL-17 production, splenocyte proliferation, and illness symptoms (Yousefi et al., 2013). On the other hand, Wang and colleagues contrasted the therapeutic effectiveness of MSCs produced from human embryos and bone marrow for the treatment of EAE. They demonstrated that, as compared to MSCs produced from bone marrow, embryonic MSCs exhibited greater therapeutic effects in reducing the severity of EAE and preventing the demyelination process. Additionally, using bone marrow MSCs to treat EAE mice was linked to IL-6 overexpression, which reduces the therapeutic effectiveness of MSCs (Wang et al., 2014). The use of genetically modified MSCs, that can generate some bioactive molecules like anti-inflammatory cytokines, is an intriguing strategy in MS therapy. According to animal models, transfecting MSCs with the neurotrophin-3 gene can dramatically boost their capacity for remyelination (Zhang et al., 2012). The symptoms of EAE have also been lessened by inoculation of MSCs expressing VIP (Cobo et al., 2013). Human adipose-derived MSCs that express IL-10 that were administered intraperitoneally to EAE mice likewise showed positive outcomes (Payne et al., 2013). It's interesting to note that giving minocycline and IFN-b secreting bone marrow-derived MSCs to EAE animals reduced inflammation, demyelination, and disease development dramatically. Additionally, intranasal treatment of MSCs that express the myelin oligodendrocyte glycoprotein-specific receptor to EAE mice was linked to increased CNS MSC infiltration and disease remission (Fransson et al., 2014).

Additionally, it has been observed that the MS mouse cuprizone model's 17β-estradiol improved the effectiveness of intravenous injection of adipose-derived MSCs in axon remyelination (Ragerdi et al., 2011). Others have observed similar findings regarding the MSCs produced from adipose's ability to ameliorate symptoms in the mouse cuprizone model (Hedayatpour et al., 2013). Unconventionally, it has been observed that neither human nor murine bone marrow-derived MSCs were able to penetrate the injured area of the mouse cuprizone model's CNS, preventing them from exerting any protective effects (Nessler et al., 2013). The ability of stem cells to alleviate EAE in mice was increased when minocycline and bone marrow-derived MSCs were administered together (Hou et al., 2013). Additionally, it has been proposed that pharmacological control of the autophagy process may intensify MSCs immunosuppressive effects in EAE mice (Dang et al., 2014). The ameliorative benefits of MSCs in the treatment of EAE involve various immunosuppressive and neuroprotective processes. It has been demonstrated that using human BM-MSCs to treat EAE can reduce IFN-c-producing cells while increasing IL-4-producing cells. Additionally, pretreatment with MSCs not only reduces the production of cytokines derived from TH1 and TH17 (like IL-17, IL-2, IL-12, IFN-c, and TNF-a), but also increases the production of cytokines derived from TH2 (like IL- 5 and IL-4) (Bai et al., 2009; Zepp et al., 2011). Additionally, it has been noted that IFN-c increases the production of a number of immunomodulatory substances by accumulating MSCs in inflammatory areas of the CNS, including IDO, TGF-β, PGE2, COX-2, and HGF (English et al., 2007). Additionally, it has been demonstrated that PGE2 produced from human BM-MSCs promotes the development of IL-10-producing anti-inflammatory macrophages (Nemeth et al., 2009). Additionally, MSCs stimulate neurogenesis by increasing macrophages' phagocytic activity, which helps them sweep away apoptotic cells (Napoli, 2010). Additionally, it has been noted that TLR3-mediated activation of MSCs in the CNS results in anti-inflammatory qualities that may be helpful in the treatment of MS and maybe EAE (Opitz et al., 2009; Auletta et al., 2010). In a recent study, it was found that MSC-CM-induced changes in cytokine expression in EAE are mediated by HGF signalling when it was administered to animals with the disease. In addition, MSC-mediated functional recovery in EAE was reduced when HGF signalling was inhibited (Bai et al., 2012). Additionally, splenocytes from EAE animals treated with MSCs were said to be less proliferative than those treated using other techniques (Bai et al., 2009). Treg cells are less common and less functional in MS patients, according to earlier research (Buckner et al., 2010). It's interesting to note that research has shown that MSCs can trigger the production of FoxP3 and increase the frequency of Treg cells both in vitro and in vivo (Bonab et al., 2011). Treatment of EAE animals with MSCs consistently slowed the disease's course and increased the mRNA for IL-10, Foxp3, TGF-b1, and Treg cells in the spleen and lymph nodes (Zhu et al., 2012). Human bone marrow-derived MSCs were intravenously injected into EAE mice, which resulted in a decrease in Th17 cells as well as an increase in the proportion of regulatory B cells (Guo et al., 2013). It's interesting to note that administration of human BM-MSCs to EAE animals enhanced oligodendrocytes and decreased astrocytes in the CNS. Given that astrocytes interfere with CNS repair and oligodendrocyte remyelination, it appears that the administration of MSCs will have ameliorative effects on MS patients (Bai et al., 2009). When mice with chronically demyelinated white matter received injections of MSCs generated from bone marrow, this consistently stimulated oligodendrocyte progenitors and accelerated the remyelination process in the transplanted area (Jaramillo et al., 2013). On the other hand, it has been demonstrated that MSCs control inflammation and apoptosis to modify astrocyte response (Sun et al., 2013). Ciliary neurotrophic factor (CNTF) and the Janus kinase/signal transducer and activator of transcription (JaK/STAT) pathway are regulated, in part, to provide this modulatory effect (Fu et al., 2014). According to some research, MSCs antioxidative function may play a role in their neuroprotective function in EAE animal models (Lanza et al., 2009). According to recent research by Kemp and colleagues, human-derived MSCs may exhibit neuroprotective effects in part by secreting superoxide dismutase 3, an extremely strong antioxidant biomolecule (Kemp et al., 2010). Additionally, it is stated that cytokines like TNF-α and IFN-c worked in concert to regulate the release of superoxide dismutase (Kemp and Gray, 2010). Additionally, it has been stated that MSCs neuroprotective effects can be attained in part by reducing the sensitivity of neurons to glutamate receptor ligands (Voulgari-Kokotaet al., 2012). Koning and colleagues recently demonstrated that the number of MSCs in the bone marrow considerably decreased during the acute phase of EAE (Koning et al., 2013). This finding shows that more MSCs migrate to the periphery during disease progression than during non-progressive illness stages. The use of MSCs in the therapy of EAE has been suggested by the immunomodulatory and neuroprotective properties noted above, as well as the ability of MSCs to move into the CNS and differentiate into neuron cells (Devine et al., 2003; Kopen et al., 1999). It has recently been demonstrated that giving adipose-derived MSCs intravenously to EAE mice prior to the onset of the illness caused the MSCs to settle in the CNS and lymphoid organs. These MSCs were then able to lessen EAE severity, demyelination, and inflammation in the brain and spinal cord (Constantin et al., 2009).

Additionally, human MSCs injected into the brain of EAE mice to stimulate the release of neurotrophic factors exhibited ameliorative effects and increased animal lifespan through the processes of immunomodulation and neuroprotection (**Fig. 14.2**) (Barhum et al., 2010). Additionally, it has been shown that administering adipose-derived MSCs to animal models of EAE reduced demyelination and axonal loss, as well as stimulated the production of TH2-type cytokines and raised the number of endogenous oligodendrocyte progenitors (Constantin et al., 2009).

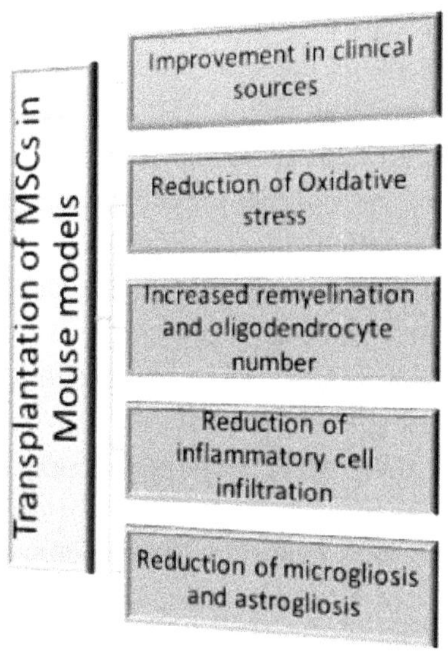

Fig. 14.2: Potential role of MSCs in mouse model of multiple sclerosis

In the first human research, *ex vivo* expanded MSCs were intrathecally injected into ten progressing MS patients. Although they did not completely succeed, it was nonetheless encouraging (Bonab et al., 2007). Another team has looked into how endometrial regenerative cells, a collection of mesenchymal-like stem cells, can help four MS patients. The cells were administered intrathecally and intravenously, and both procedures exhibited ameliorative benefits (Zhong et al., 2009). Immunosuppression and disease attenuation were also linked to giving umbilical cord-derived

MSCs to MS patients (Liang et al., 2009).The intrathecal administration of ex vivo generated autologous bone marrow produced MSCs to ten MS patients was recently reported by Yamout et al. to exhibit ameliorative effects (Yamout et al., 2010).

With the use of intrathecal and intravenous delivery of autologous MSCs, Karussis and colleagues conducted a phase 1/2 open safety clinical research in 15 MS patients and demonstrated immunomodulatory effects of MSCs as well as their safety in MS therapy (Karussis et al., 2010).The feasibility, safety, and effectiveness of using autologous MSCs in 10 SPMS patients have also been demonstrated by another phase IIA trial (Connick et al., 2011). Additionally, the treatment of fifty MS patients in Iraq with intrathecal injections of peripheral blood cells purified using aphaeresis after G-CSF (granulocyte colony stimulating factor) therapy was linked to encouraging outcomes (Hammadi et al., 2011). Consistently, the findings of a clinical trial research conducted by Connick and colleagues, in which ten SPMS patients with optic nerve deficits received intravenously administered doses of autologous MSCs while being closely monitored for ten months, have just been published. These patients' optic nerves seemed to be recovering somewhat, and using MSCs didn't seem to have any negative side effects (Connick et al., 2012). Eight MS patients had an intravenous infusion of autologous MSCs, and there were some good side effects but no major negative ones (Odinak et al., 2010). Twenty-five progressive MS patients who were unresponsive to conventional treatments were also studied for the ameliorative effects of MSC transplantation by Bonab and colleagues, who demonstrated that an intrathecal infusion of ex vivo expanded MSCs attenuated disease symptoms without having a significant negative impact (Mohyeddin Bonab et al., 2012). Additionally, it has been shown that treating MS patients with MSCs intravenously causes FoxP3 to be upregulated in PBMCs (Mohajeri et al., 2011). On the other hand, it has been shown that injecting MSCs intrathecally into 25 MS patients had no impact on peripheral blood levels of cytokines like IFN-c, TGF-b, IL-4, IL-10, IL-6, and FoxP3. According to the authors, the local function of MSCs in the CNS is what is responsible for this variation (Mohyeddin Bonab et al., 2013).

Furthermore, no notable side effects were seen during the four years when one MS patient with progressing disease was treated with both allogenic human umbilical cord-derived MSCs and autologous bone marrow-derived MSCs (Hou et al., 2013).The efficacy and side effects of treating MS patients with MSCs are the subject of numerous ongoing clinical trials taking place in various parts of the world (Joyce et al., 2010).

Disadvantages of the application of MSCs

The inability to effectively distinguish between the immune reaction against infections and the immunological response against bodily tissues in autoimmune illness is the fundamental drawback of utilising immunosuppressive medicines. As a result, the host immune system is suppressed by these drugs, which reduces the immune system's ability to fight against diseases and viruses. Fortunately, because MSCs can move into inflammatory tissues, their immunosuppressive activity is only present in inflammatory areas. Nevertheless, despite the aforementioned benefits, there are some worries regarding the MSCs' capacity to generate ectopic tissues as well as the possibility of their transformation and tumorigenic potential (Garcia et al., 2008; Gugjoo, 2022).

Conclusion

MSCs have received a great deal of attention over the past ten years.The usage of MSC has led to the development of a novel therapeutic strategy for autoimmune diseases. MSCs are being routinely used in clinical trials, and preliminary positive findings have been observed in terms of MS management and treatment. But it's hard to narrow down exactly how MSCs function to make things better. Numerous studies have shown that in different inflammatory organs, MSCs interact closely with a variety of immune cells and chemicals. As a result, they may serve as useful tools in the treatment of numerous inflammatory illnesses, including MS. Here, we gave a summary of what is currently known regarding the clinical uses of MSCs in MS. Additionally, the principal difficulties and dangers of MSCs therapy in MS patients have been clarified.To effectively treat MS patients, it is vital to pinpoint their particular mechanisms.

Future research into these pathways may aid in choosing the appropriate injection dose and timing, as well as the best MSC type from different source tissues, for each stage of MS.In studies employing multiple sclerosis animal models, mesenchymal stem cells affected both innate and adaptive immunity.

References

1. Alchi B, et al. (2013). Autologous haematopoietic stem cell transplantation for systemic lupus erythematosus: data from the European Group for Blood and Marrow Transplantation registry. Lupus

22: 245–253.

2. Atkins HL, & Freedman MS. (2017). Five questions answered: a review of autologous hematopoietic stem cell transplantation for the treatment of multiple sclerosis. Neurotherapeutics 14: 888–893.
3. Auletta JJ, et al. (2010). Regenerative stromal cell therapy in allogeneic hematopoietic stem cell transplantation: current impact and future directions, Biol. Blood Marrow Transplant 16(7): 891–906.
4. Bai L, et al. (2009). Human bone marrow-derived mesenchymal stem cells induce Th2-polarized immune response and promote endogenous repair in animal models of multiple sclerosis, Glia 57 (11): 1192–1203.
5. Bai L, et al. (2012). Hepatocyte growth factor mediates mesenchymal stem cell-induced recovery in multiple sclerosis models. Nat Neurosci 15: 862–870.
6. Bai L, et al. (2012). Hepatocyte growth factor mediates mesenchymal stem cell-induced recovery in multiple sclerosis models, Nat Neurosci 15(6): 862–870.
7. Barhum Y, et al. (2010). Intracerebroventricular transplantation of human mesenchymal stem cells induced to secrete neurotrophic factors attenuates clinical symptoms in a mouse model of multiple sclerosis. J Mol Neurosci 41(1): 129–137.
8. Bonab JM. FOXP3 gene expression in multiple sclerosis patients pre-and post-mesenchymal stem cell therapy. Iran J Allergy Asthma Immunol 10(3): (2011).
9. Bonab M, et al. (2012). Autologous mesenchymal stem cell therapy in progressive multiple sclerosis: an open label study. Curr Stem Cell Res Ther 7(6): 407–414.
10. Bonab MM, et al. (2007). Does mesenchymal stem cell therapy help multiple sclerosis patients? Report of a pilot study Iran J Immunol 4(1): 50–57.
11. Bonab MM, et al. (2013). Evaluation of cytokines in multiple sclerosis patients treated with mesenchymal stem cells. Arch Med Res 44(4): 266–272.
12. Bosca I, et al. (2008). Effect of relapses over early progression of disability in multiple sclerosis patients treated with beta-interferon. Mult Scler 14: 636–639.
13. Buckner JH (2010). Mechanisms of impaired regulation by CD4+ CD25+ FOXP3+ regulatory T cells in human autoimmune diseases. Nat Rev Immunol 10(12) 849–859.

14. Cobo M, et al. (2013). Mesenchymal stem cells expressing vasoactive intestinal peptide ameliorate symptoms in a model of chronic multiple sclerosis, Cell Transplant 22(5): 839–854.
15. Cohen JA, et al. (2018). Pilot trial of intravenous autologous cultureexpanded mesenchymal stem cell transplantation in multiple sclerosis. Mult Scler 24: 501–511.
16. Confavreux C, & Vukusic S. (2006). Natural history of multiple sclerosis: a unifying concept. Brain 129: 606–616.
17. Connick P, et al. (2011). The mesenchymal stem cells in multiple sclerosis (MSCIMS) trial protocol and baseline cohort characteristics: an open-label pre-test: post-test study with blinded outcome assessments. Trials 12(1): 62.
18. Connick P, et al. (2012). Autologous mesenchymal stem cells for the treatment of secondary progressive multiple sclerosis: an open-label phase 2a proof-of-concept study. Lancet Neurol 11: 150–156.
19. Connick P, et al. (2012). Autologous mesenchymal stem cells for the treatment of secondary progressive multiple sclerosis: an open-label phase 2a proof-of-concept study. Lancet Neurol 11(2): 150–156.
20. Constantin G, et al. (2009). Adipose-derived mesenchymal stem cells ameliorate chronic experimental autoimmune encephalomyelitis, Stem Cells 27(10): 2624–2635.
21. Dahbour S, et al. (2017). Mesenchymal stem cells and conditioned media in the treatment of multiple sclerosis patients: clinical, ophthalmological and radiological assessments of safety and efficacy. CNS Neurosci Ther 23: 866–874.
22. Dang S, et al. (2014). Autophagy regulates the therapeutic potential of mesenchymal stem cells in experimental autoimmune encephalomyelitis, Autophagy 10(7): 62–71.
23. De Paula ASA, et al. (2015). Autologous haematopoieticstem cell transplantation reduces abnormalities in the expression of immune genes in multiple sclerosis. Clin. Sci (Lond.) 128: 111–120.
24. Devine SM, et al. (2003). Mesenchymal stem cells distribute to a wide range of tissues following systemic infusion into nonhuman primates, Blood 101(8): 2999–3001.
25. English K, et al. (2007). IFN-gamma and TNFalpha differentially regulate immunomodulation by murine mesenchymal stem cells. Immunol Lett 110(2): 91–100.

26. Fisher-Shoval Y, et al. (2012). Transplantation of placenta-derived mesenchymal stem cells in the EAE mouse model of MS. J Mol Neurosci 48(1): 176–184.
27. Fransson M, et al. (2014). Intranasal delivery of CNS-retargeted human mesenchymal stromal cells prolongs treatment efficacy of experimental autoimmune encephalomyelitis. Immunol 142(3): 431-41.
28. Freedman MS, et al. (2010). The therapeutic potential of mesenchymal stem cell transplantation as a treatment for multiple sclerosis: consensus report of the International MSCT Study Group. Mult Scler 16: 503–510.
29. Fu XM, et al. (2014). Combined bone mesenchymal stem cells and olfactory ensheathing cells transplantation promote neural repair associated with CNTF expression in traumatic brain injured rats. Cell Transplant 24(8): 1533-44
30. Garcia-Castro J, et al. (2008). Mesenchymal stem cells and their use as cell replacement therapy and disease modelling tool. J Cell Mol Med 12(6b): 2552– 2565.
31. Genc B, et al. (2019). Stem cell therapy for multiple sclerosis. Adv Exp Med Biol 1084:145–174.
32. Gerdoni E, et al. (2007). Mesenchymal stem cells effectively modulate pathogenic immune response in experimental autoimmune encephalomyelitis, Ann Neurol 61(3): 219–227.
33. Gordon D, et al. (2008). Human mesenchymal stem cells abrogate experimental allergic encephalomyelitis after intraperitoneal injection, and with sparse CNS infiltration, Neurosci Lett 448(1): 71–73.
34. Grigoriadis N, et al. (2011). Variable behavior and complications of autologous bone marrow mesenchymal stem cells transplanted in experimental autoimmune encephalomyelitis, Exp Neurol 230(1): 78–89.
35. Gugjoo MB. (2022). Mesenchymal Stem Cells Therapeutic Applications in Central Nervous System Disorders. In: Therapeutic Applications of Mesenchymal Stem Cells in Veterinary Medicine. Springer Nature. pp. 163-212.
36. Guo Y, et al. (2013). Human mesenchymal stem cells upregulate CD1dhighCD5+ regulatory B cells in experimental autoimmune encephalomyelitis, NeuroImmunoModulation, 20(5): 294–303.
37. Hammadi AMA, et al. (2011). Clinical outcome of 50 progressive multiple sclerosis patients treated with cellular therapy in Iraq. Int J Stem Cells 4(2): 113.

38. Harris VK, et al. (2012). Characterization of autologous mesenchymal stem cell-derived neural progenitors as a feasible source of stem cells for central nervous system applications in multiple sclerosis, Stem Cells Transl Med 1(7): 536–547.
39. Harris VK, et al. (2012). Clinical and pathological effects of intrathecal injection of mesenchymal stem cellderived neural progenitors in an experimental model of multiple sclerosis. J Neurol Sci 313(1): 167–177.
40. Harris VK, et al. (2018). Phase I trial of intrathecal mesenchymal stem cell-derived neural progenitors in progressive multiple sclerosis. EBioMedicine 29: 23–30.
41. Hedayatpour A, et al. (2013). Promotion of remyelination by adipose mesenchymal stem cell transplantation in a cuprizone model of multiple sclerosis, Cell J. (Yakhteh) 15(2): 142.
42. Hou Y, et al. (2013). Effective combination of human bone marrow mesenchymal stem cells and minocycline in experimental autoimmune encephalomyelitis mice, Stem Cell Res Ther 4(4): 77.
43. Hou Z-I, et al. (2013). Transplantation of umbilical cord and bone marrow-derived mesenchymal stem cells in a patient with relapsing-remitting multiple sclerosis. Cell Adhes Migr 7(5): 404.
44. Jaramillo-Merchan J, et al. (2013). Mesenchymal stromal-cell transplants induce oligodendrocyte progenitor migration and remyelination in a chronic demyelination model, Cell Death Dis 4(8): e779.
45. Joyce G, et al. (2010). Mesenchymal stem cells for the treatment of neurodegenerative disease. Regen Med 5(6): 933–946.
46. Karussis D, et al. (2010). Safety and immunological effects of mesenchymal stem cell transplantation in patients with multiple sclerosis and amyotrophic lateral sclerosis. Arch Neurol 67(10): 1187–1194.
47. Kemp K, et al. (2010). Inflammatory cytokine induced regulation of superoxide dismutase 3 expression by human mesenchymal stem cells. Stem Cell Rev Rep 6(4): 548–559.
48. Kemp K, et al. (2010). Mesenchymal stem cell-secreted superoxide dismutase promotes cerebellar neuronal survival. J Neurochem 114(6): 1569–1580.
49. Kemp K, et al. (2011). Fusion between human mesenchymal stem cells and rodent cerebellar Purkinje cells, Neuropathol Appl Neurobiol 37(2): 166–178.

50. Koning JJ, (2013). Mesenchymal stem cells are mobilized from the bone marrow during inflammation. Front Immunol 4: 49.
51. Kopen GC, et al. (1999). Marrow stromal cells migrate throughout forebrain and cerebellum, and they differentiate into astrocytes after injection into neonatal mouse brains, Proc Natl Acad Sci 96(19): 10711–10716.
52. Lanza C, et al. (2009). Neuroprotective mesenchymal stem cells are endowed with a potent antioxidant effect in vivo. J Neurochem 110(5): 1674–1684.
53. Li XL, et al. (2014). Atorvastatin calcium in combination with methylprednisolone for the treatment of multiple sclerosis relapse. Int Immunopharmacol 23: 546–549.
54. Liang J, et al. (2009). Allogeneic mesenchymal stem cells transplantation in treatment of multiple sclerosis. Mult Scler 15(5): 644–646.
55. Liu R, et al. (2012). Human umbilical cord stem cells ameliorate experimental autoimmune encephalomyelitis by regulating immunoinflammation and remyelination, Stem Cells Dev 22(7): 1053–1062.
56. Lotfy A, et al. (2020). Mesenchymal stem cells as a treatment for multiple sclerosis: a focus on experimental animal studies. Rev Neurosci 31(2): 161-179.
57. Lunn JS, et al. (2014). Concise review: stem cell therapies for amyotrophic lateral sclerosis: recent advances and prospects for the future. Stem Cells 32: 1099–1109.
58. Meamar R, et al. (2016). The role of stem cell therapy in multiple sclerosis: an overview of the current status of the clinical studies. Adv Biomed. Res 5: 46.
59. Mohajeri M, et al. (2011). FOXP3 gene expression in multiple sclerosis patients pre-and post mesenchymal stem cell therapy. Iran J Allergy Asthma Immunol 10(3): 155–161.
60. Napoli I, & Neumann H. (2010). Protective effects of microglia in multiple sclerosis, Exp Neurol 225(1): 24–28.
61. Nemeth K, et al. (2009). Bone marrow stromal cells attenuate sepsis via prostaglandin E[2]- dependent reprogramming of host macrophages to increase their interleukin-10 production. Nat Med 15(1): 42–49.
62. Nessler J, et al. (2013). Effects of murine and human bone marrow-derived mesenchymal stem cells on cuprizone induced demyelination, PLoS One 8(7) e69795.

63. Odinak G, et al. (2010). Transplantation of mesenchymal stem cells in multiple sclerosis. Zh Nevrol Psikhiatr Im S S Korsakova 111(2 Pt 2): 72–76.
64. Opitz CA, et al. (2009). Toll-like receptor engagement enhances the immunosuppressive properties of human bone marrow-derived mesenchymal stem cells by inducing indoleamine-2, 3-dioxygenase-1 via interferon-b and protein kinase R. Stem Cells 27(4): 909–919.
65. Orack JC, et al. (2015). Concise review: modeling multiple sclerosis with stem cell biological platforms: toward functional validation of cellular and molecular phenotypes in inflammation-induced neurodegeneration. Stem Cells Transl Med 4: 252–260.
66. Payne NL, et al. (2013). Human adipose-derived mesenchymal stem cells engineered to secrete IL-10 inhibit APC function and limit CNS autoimmunity, Brain Behav Immun 30: 103–114.
67. Racosta JM, & Kimpinski K. (2016). Autonomic dysfunction, immune regulation, and multiple sclerosis. Clin Auton Res 26: 23–31.
68. Rafei M, et al. (2009). Allogeneic mesenchymal stem cells for treatment of experimental autoimmune encephalomyelitis, Mol Ther 17(10): 1799–1803.
69. Ragerdi KI, et al. (2011). 17b-Estradiol enhances the efficacy of adipose-derived mesenchymal stem cells on remyelination in mouse model of multiple sclerosis, Acta Med Iran 50(12): 789–797.
70. Riordan NH, et al. (2018). Clinical feasibility of umbilical cord tissuederived mesenchymal stem cells in the treatment of multiple sclerosis. J Transl Med 16: 57.
71. Schafer R, et al (2008). The use of clinically approved small particles of iron oxide (SPIO) for labelling of mesenchymal stem cells aggravates clinical symptoms in experimental autoimmune encephalomyelitis and influences their in vivo distribution, Cell Transplant 17(8): 923–941.
72. Strong AL, et al. (2016). Human adipose stromal stem cells from obese donors show reduced efficacy in halting disease progression in the experimental autoimmune encephalomyelitis model of multiple sclerosis. Stem Cells 34: 614–626.
73. Sun H, et al. (2013). Therapeutic potential of mesenchymal stromal cells and MSC conditioned medium in amyotrophic lateral sclerosis (ALS)-in vitro evidence from primary motor neuron cultures, NSC-34 cells, astrocytes and microglia, PLoS One 8(9): e72926.

74. Tafreshi AP, et al. (2014). Bernard, Inactive GSK3b is disturbed in the spinal cord during experimental autoimmune encephalomyelitis, but rescued by stem cell therapy. Neurosci 277: 498-505.
75. Voulgari-Kokota A, et al. (2012). Mesenchymal stem cells protect CNS neurons against glutamate excitotoxicity by inhibiting glutamate receptor expression and function. Exp Neurol 236(1): 161–170.
76. Walczak A, et al. (2013). Transdermal application of myelin peptides in multiple sclerosis treatment. JAMA Neurol 70: 1105–1109.
77. Walczak A, et al. (2013). Transdermal application of myelin peptides in multiple sclerosis treatment. JAMA Neurol. 70: 1105–1109.
78. Wang X, et al. (2014). Human ESC-Derived MSCs Outperform Bone Marrow MSCs in the Treatment of an EAE Model of Multiple Sclerosis. Stem Cell Rep 3(1):115-30.
79. Yamout B, et al. (2010). Bone marrow mesenchymal stem cell transplantation in patients with multiple sclerosis: a pilot study. J Neuroimmunol 227(1): 185–189.
80. Yousefi F, et al. (2013). Comparison of in vivo immunomodulatory effects of intravenous and intraperitoneal administration of adipose-tissue mesenchymal stem cells in experimental autoimmune encephalomyelitis (EAE), Int Immunopharmacol 17(3): 608–616.
81. Yousefi F, et al. (2016). *In vivo* immunomodulatory effects of adiposederived mesenchymal stem cells conditioned medium in experimental autoimmune encephalomyelitis. Immunol Lett 172: 94–105.
82. Zappia E, et al. (2005). Mesenchymal stem cells ameliorate experimental autoimmune encephalomyelitis inducing T-cell anergy, Blood 106(5): 1755–1761.
83. Zepp J. et al. (2011). IL-17 receptor signaling and T helper 17-mediated autoimmune demyelinating disease. Trends Immunol 32(5): 232– 239.
84. Zhang Y-J, et al. (2012). Neurotrophin-3 gene modified mesenchymal stem cells promote remyelination and functional recovery in the demyelinated spinal cord of rats, J Neurol Sci 313(1): 64–74.
85. Zhong Z, et al. (2009). Feasibility investigation of allogeneic endometrial regenerative cells. J Transl Med 7(15): 29–37.
86. Zhu J, et al. (2012. Transplanting of mesenchymal stem cells may affect proliferation and function of CD4 (+) T cells in experimental autoimmune encephalomyelitis. Exp Clin Transpl 10(5): 492–500.

www.ingramcontent.com/pod-product-compliance
Ingram Content Group UK Ltd.
Pitfield, Milton Keynes, MK11 3LW, UK
UKHW021915190726
13853UKWH00002B/688